UNDERV

RESURREC ⎯⎯⎯⎯ ...NGDOM

Books by David H.J.Gay referred to in this volume:

Baptist Sacramentalism: A Warning to Baptists.

Battle for the Church: 1517-1644.

Christ Is All: No Sanctification by the Law.

Christ's Obedience Imputed.

Clearing the Smoke: Matthew 5 Reclaimed.

Conversion Ruined: The New Perspective and the Conversion of Sinners.

Evangelicals Warned: Isaiah 30 Speaks Today.

Fivefold Sanctification.

In Church or In Christ?

Infant Baptism Tested.

Liberty Not Licence.

Man: His Uniqueness, Ruin and Redemption.

Relationship Evangelism Exposed: A Blight on the Churches and the Ungodly.

Romans 11: A Suggested Exegesis.

Sowed Much, Reaped Little: Why?: The Sermon: The Gap between the Claim and the Result.

The Evangelical Dilemma: Evangelistic Addresses (Apostolic and Modern) Compared.

The Hinge in Romans 1 – 8: A critique of N.T.Wright's view of Baptism and Conversion.

The Priesthood of All Believers: Slogan or Substance?

To Confront or Not to Confront?: Addresses to Unbelievers.

Undervalued Themes

Resurrection and Kingdom

If Christ has not been raised, then our preaching is in vain and your faith is in vain. We are even found to be misrepresenting God, because we testified about God that he raised Christ, whom he did not raise if it is true that the dead are not raised. For if the dead are not raised, not even Christ has been raised. And if Christ has not been raised, your faith is futile and you are still in your sins. Then those also who have fallen asleep in Christ have perished. If in Christ we have hope in this life only, we are of all people most to be pitied. But in fact Christ has been raised from the dead, the firstfruits of those who have fallen asleep. For as by a man came death, by a man has come also the resurrection of the dead.

1 Corinthians 15:14-21

Jesus, remember me when you come into your kingdom.

Luke 23:42

...our blessed hope, the appearing of the glory of our great God and Saviour Jesus Christ.

Titus 2:13

These men who have turned the world upside down have come here also... acting against the decrees of Caesar, saying that there is another king, Jesus.

Acts 17:6-7

David H.J.Gay

BRACHUS

BRACHUS 2023
davidhjgay@googlemail.com

Scripture quotations come from a variety of versions

Contents

Introduction

Titles are tricky. At least, for me. I want them to be snappy, arousing some interest, giving an idea of what to expect – things not always easy to reconcile. Back in the old days, quite often the title itself was a minor booklet. Subtitles, I find, come to the rescue. A bit.

The two 'undervalued themes' in the title are, as the subtitle makes clear, Christ's resurrection (leading to the believer's resurrection) and Christ's kingdom. (As a working definition, I take this 'kingdom' to be the time of Christ's reign, Christ as King, the final overthrow of evil, and the ultimate triumph of God and his people). These two themes – resurrection and kingdom – are, in my view, undervalued by most believers today; they seem to border on being non-issues for them. About twenty years ago, a lady of my vintage told me how refreshing it was to hear a discourse on the Second Coming: 'We never hear it these days!' Is it because, unlike the early believers, we have become comfortable in this world?[1]

I say 'undervalued', but this needs a more nuanced explanation, especially with regard to 'kingdom'. Some sections of Christendom make much of 'kingdom', but do so in terms of church-triumphalism, or the wielding of political power by the church for revolution or social improvement, or the saving of the planet from environmental destruction, and so on.[2] William Blake's *Jerusalem* encapsulates one aspect of it:

---

[1] In my early days as a believer (mid to late 1950s), the second coming of Christ was a much-discussed subject, arousing much passion. Alas, the group I belonged to was pre-occupied with fitting Middle-Eastern political events and personalities into Scripture. Nevertheless, we were, at least in this regard, interested in Christ's return.

[2] See, for example, N.T.Wright: *The Resurrection of the Son of God*, SPCK, London, 2003. See also the final chapters of Sharon James: *How Christianity Transformed the World*, Christian Focus Publications, Fearn, 2021 and *The Lies We Are Told...,* Christian Focus

And did those feet in ancient time
Walk upon England's mountains green:
And was the holy Lamb of God,
On England's pleasant pastures seen!

And did the countenance divine,
Shine forth upon our clouded hills?
And was Jerusalem builded here,
Among these dark satanic mills?

Bring me my bow of burning gold:
Bring me my arrows of desire:
Bring me my spear: O clouds unfold!
Bring me my chariot of fire!

I will not cease from mental fight,
Nor shall my sword sleep in my hand:
Till we have built Jerusalem,
In England's green & pleasant land.

This is not what Scripture means by the kingdom of Christ.

Confusion over the kingdom is nothing new. Christ met it in his day. He not only met it; he confronted it head-on. The prophets had repeatedly spoken of the coming Messiah, the King, the one who would establish his kingdom, and many Jews of Christ's day were looking out for the fulfilment of those prophecies (Luke 1:67-79; 2:25-38; 23:51, for instance).[3] This expectation, and curiosity about it, was longstanding. Christ told his disciples:

> Blessed are the eyes that see what you see! For I tell you that many prophets and kings desired to see what you see, and did not see it, and to hear what you hear, and did not hear it (Luke 10:23-24).

Publications, Fearn, 2022, for post-millennialism based on old-covenant texts, heyday-Puritan prophetical dreams (ignoring late Puritans who had to live with defeat), Jonathan Edwards, selective C.H.Spurgeon, and (very heavily) on Iain Murray: *The Puritan Hope*, Banner of Truth Trust, Edinburgh, 1971. For my brief reply, see Appendix 1.
[3] See my series of sermons 'The Watershed of the Ages' on my sermonaudio.com page.

Peter could later write:

> Concerning this salvation, the prophets who prophesied about
> the grace that was to be yours searched and inquired carefully,
> inquiring what person or time the Spirit of Christ in them was
> indicating when he predicted the sufferings of Christ and the
> subsequent glories. It was revealed to them that they were
> serving not themselves but you, in the things that have now
> been announced to you through those who preached the good
> news to you by the Holy Spirit sent from heaven, things into
> which angels long to look (1 Pet. 1:10-12).

So far, so good. But the Jews of Christ's day were expecting
those prophecies to be fulfilled in the restoration of something
very like Solomon's kingdom, a resurgence of the temple, a
glorious nation arising out of deliverance from Roman
occupation, that humiliation which had lasted for well-nigh a
century. These dreams were wild, badly mistaken, and Christ
told them so. Take, for example, his kingdom-parables of
Matthew 13: the kingdom would not be a renewed Jewish
kingdom like Solomon's: indeed, it wouldn't be Jewish, at all.
The kingdom would be taken from the Jews and given to others
(Matt. 21:43)! How wrong could these Jews be!

Other Jews thought of the kingdom in terms of material
prosperity. They, too, were wrong. Facing the crowds who were
flocking to him after his miraculous feeding of the thousands,
Jesus, knowing what was in their minds and hearts, preached
what might well be considered his most challenging sermon –
on the necessity of eating his flesh and drinking his blood:

> Perceiving then that they were about to come and take him by
> force to make him king, Jesus withdrew again to the mountain
> by himself... The next day... Jesus [told] them: 'Truly, truly, I
> say to you, you are seeking me, not because you saw signs, but
> because you ate your fill of the loaves' (John 6:15,22,26).

With these words, Christ launched into his devastating
discourse, a discourse which had dramatic consequences, with
thousands turning away from him, determined to have nothing
more to do with him. If he wasn't going to be a material Santa
Claus handing out goodies right, left and centre, if he was

unequivocally demanding spiritual life, if that was what it was all about, goodbye!

Again, take John 8. When Christ told the Jews that they were slaves, they, thinking in political, economic and social terms, deeply offended by his remarks, responded with vigour:

> We are offspring of Abraham and have never been enslaved to anyone. How is it that you say: 'You will become free'?

Never enslaved to anyone? How could they say such a thing? They knew full well that, even as they were loud in their protest and denial, they were under the power of Rome (John 11:48; 18:31), and had been, as I say, for a century.

In any case, Christ immediately disabused them. As he explained, membership of his kingdom would spell freedom from the true and eternal slavery; slavery to the devil and sin, not slavery to the Romans, or whatever, is the real bondage gripping men:

> If you abide in my word, you are truly my disciples, and you will know the truth, and the truth will set you free... Truly, truly, I say to you, everyone who practices sin is a slave to sin... If the Son sets you free, you will be free indeed (John 8:31-36).

It was not just the unbelieving Jews who were mistaken about the kingdom – even Christ's own disciples, those who had been with him throughout his ministry, could think of the kingdom in no other way than the restoration of the majesty of Solomon's day, the restoration of Israel's military, political and economic power, with the overthrow of the Roman occupation.[4] Take the way the two on the Emmaus road opened their hearts to their

---

[4] Earthly kingship in Christ's day meant a culture of despotism and tyranny – more like Germany under Hitler and Russia under Stalin. In the West, we have virtually lost the concept of kingship which was current in Christ's day. In the UK, we have had a constitutional monarchy (virtually toothless) for over 300 years. The US threw off even constitutional monarchy in the late 18th century.

unrecognised companion, explaining why they were so depressed:

> Jesus of Nazareth, a man who was a prophet mighty in deed and word before God and all the people... our chief priests and rulers delivered him up to be condemned to death, and crucified him. But we had hoped that he was the one to redeem Israel. Yes, and besides all this, it is now the third day since these things happened.

By 'the redemption of Israel' they did not mean 'salvation from sin'; they meant the triumph of the Messiah in his restoration of the kingdom for Israel, the renaissance of the temple, and deliverance of the nation from Roman captivity. Despite the plain and repeated teaching that Christ had given them about his sufferings (Luke 9:21-22,43-45; 13:33; 18:31-34; 22:15, for instance), they simply could not shake off their triumphalist expectations. Christ's response on the Emmaus road was blunt: his kingdom was not one of old-covenant kingly and priestly power and display, nor of military and economic prowess, but quite the opposite.[5] His kingdom would be one of weakness, of suffering, of rejection. Indeed, shocking as it must have sounded, the Messiah – he, himself – had come to die:

> O foolish ones, and slow of heart to believe all that the prophets have spoken! Was it not necessary that the Christ should suffer these things and enter into his glory?... And beginning with Moses and all the prophets, he interpreted to

---

[5] For instance: 'Many who are first will be last, and the last first' (Matt. 19:30). 'The greatest among you shall be your servant. Whoever exalts himself will be humbled, and whoever humbles himself will be exalted' (Matt. 23:11-12). 'If I then, your Lord and Teacher, have washed your feet, you also ought to wash one another's feet. For I have given you an example, that you also should do just as I have done to you. Truly, truly, I say to you, a servant is not greater than his master, nor is a messenger greater than the one who sent him' (John 13:14-16). 'God chose what is foolish in the world to shame the wise; God chose what is weak in the world to shame the strong; God chose what is low and despised in the world, even things that are not, to bring to nothing things that are, so that no human being might boast in the presence of God' (1 Cor. 1:27-29). And so on.

them in all the Scriptures the things concerning himself (Luke 24:19-27).

But, as they listened to the truth he unfolded, their cloud of depression lifted:

Did not our hearts burn within us while he talked to us on the road, while he opened to us the Scriptures? (Luke 24:32).

As Christ later explained to his gathered disciples, real kingdom work – which was what they were going to be engaged in – would be very different to the old covenant:

[Christ] said to them: 'These are my words that I spoke to you while I was still with you, that everything written about me in the law of Moses and the prophets and the psalms must be fulfilled'. Then he opened their minds to understand the Scriptures, and said to them: 'Thus it is written, that the Christ should suffer and on the third day rise from the dead, and that repentance for the forgiveness of sins should be proclaimed in his name to all nations, beginning from Jerusalem. You are witnesses of these things. And behold, I am sending the promise of my Father upon you. But stay in the city until you are clothed with power from on high' (Luke 24:44-49).[6]

This, of course, was all of a piece with Christ's great commission:

All authority in heaven and on earth has been given to me. Go therefore and make disciples of all nations, baptising them in the name of the Father and of the Son and of the Holy Spirit, teaching them to observe all that I have commanded you. And behold, I am with you always, to the end of the age (Matt. 28:18-20).

---

[6] Indeed, as already noted, Christ had long since told the Jewish leaders, his kingdom would not a Jewish affair: 'The kingdom of God will be taken away from you and given to a people producing its fruits' (Matt. 21:43). Christ, of course, was referring to the body of believers (1 Pet. 2:9-10). The AV's 'The kingdom of God shall be taken from you, and given to a nation bringing forth the fruits thereof' must not be interpreted as a reference to England, Scotland or America. As before, see my *Battle* for the very costly consequences of that foolish mistake.

Go into all the world and proclaim the gospel to the whole creation. Whoever believes and is baptised will be saved, but whoever does not believe will be condemned (Mark 16:15-16).

Instead of conquest through victory in war (Ex. 23:20-30; Num. 33:50-53l; Josh. 10:14,42, for instance), in the new covenant the aim would be the glory of God in the conversion of sinners. Of course, without trust in Christ sinners would perish, but these last days would be the days of John 3:16. That would be kingdom work.

Nevertheless, even after such clear explanations, during the days leading up to Pentecost, Christ still had to disabuse his disciples about the kingdom:

> He presented himself alive to them after his suffering by many proofs, appearing to them during forty days and speaking about the kingdom of God (Acts 1:3).

He gave them strict instructions accompanied by a promise of enormous importance:

> [Christ] ordered them not to depart from Jerusalem, but to wait for the promise of the Father, which, he said: 'You heard from me; for John baptised with water, but you will be baptised with the Holy Spirit not many days from now' (Acts 1:4-5).

And still the disciples could not let go of their mistaken ideas:

> So when they had come together, they asked him: 'Lord, will you at this time restore the kingdom to Israel?' (Acts 1:6).

So, yet again, Christ set them on the right course:

> He said to them: 'It is not for you to know times or seasons that the Father has fixed by his own authority. But you will receive power when the Holy Spirit has come upon you, and you will be my witnesses in Jerusalem and in all Judea and Samaria, and to the end of the earth' (Acts 1:7-8).

As we continue to read on in Acts, we see that the penny finally dropped. Take James' words at the *ekklēsia* meeting in

Jerusalem,[7] called to discuss issues raised by the advance of the gospel – the advance of the kingdom – among the Gentiles; they are very significant in showing how the believers had come to re-interpret the prophets:

> Simeon has related how God first visited the Gentiles, to take from them a people for his name. And with this the words of the prophets agree, just as it is written: 'After this I will return, and I will rebuild the tent of David that has fallen; I will rebuild its ruins, and I will restore it, that the remnant of mankind may seek the Lord, and all the Gentiles who are called by my name, says the Lord, who makes these things known from of old' (Acts 15:14-18, quoting Amos 9:11-12).

In short, Christ's kingdom is utterly different to any and every earthly kingdom. At this point, Daniel 2 should be read, culminating in:

> In the days of those kings the God of heaven will set up a kingdom that shall never be destroyed, nor shall the kingdom be left to another people. It shall break in pieces all these kingdoms and bring them to an end, and it shall stand forever, just as you saw that a stone was cut from a mountain by no human hand, and that it broke in pieces the iron, the bronze, the clay, the silver, and the gold. A great God has made known to the king what shall be after this. The dream is certain, and its interpretation sure (Dan. 2:44-45).

The Lord's classic statement before Pilate should have settled the issue once and for all:

> My kingdom is not of this world. If my kingdom were of this world, my servants would have been fighting, that I might not be delivered over to the Jews. But my kingdom is not from the world (John 18:36).

Yet, notwithstanding all this weight of teaching and experience, years later Paul still found it necessary to correct the Corinthian believers over the way the kingdom would be advanced:

---

[7] A meeting of the Jerusalem *ekklēsia*, please note, not a Church Council (talk about reading back into Scripture!) (see my *Battle*).

I beg of you that when I am present I may not have to show boldness with such confidence as I count on showing against some who suspect us of walking according to the flesh. For though we walk in the flesh, we are not waging war according to the flesh. For the weapons of our warfare are not of the flesh but have divine power to destroy strongholds. We destroy arguments and every lofty opinion raised against the knowledge of God, and take every thought captive to obey Christ, being ready to punish every disobedience, when your obedience is complete (2 Cor. 10:2-6).

I leave it there – for now. All I wanted to do at this stage was to make the case that mistakes over the kingdom are nothing new. Such misunderstanding seems almost endemic among believers. And that misunderstanding – or, to add yet another ingredient to the mix – that neglect of the theme of the kingdom, is part of the background to the publishing of this present work.[8]

As for the second 'theme' – resurrection – I am not neutral; I take the biblical account of Christ's physical resurrection for granted. Moreover, I do not try to bring the witnesses' accounts into a simple order, nor do I set about providing evidence to support those accounts.[9] There is no shortage of material for those who wish to pursue such questions, but I am concerned with looking at what the Bible says about the way Christ's resurrection affected, changed – turned upside down, more like – the lives of the first believers: how the resurrection revolutionised the way they thought, how they lived, how and what they preached, and the hope it gave them when facing bereavement and death. No mean list!

---

[8] For all their many errors, Jehovah Witnesses with their 'kingdom hall' put to shame those evangelicals who describe their meeting house as 'a church'.

[9] Just to say in passing, the variety in the witnesses' accounts, far from damaging their testimony, is perfectly natural and serves only to strengthen it. It is just what we would expect – and get – when several witnesses testify about a road accident, for instance. What is more, if all the witnesses of the resurrection had given precisely the same account in exact detail, the cry of 'Conspiracy!' would brought the plaster from the ceiling!

What is more, I do not write in any antiquarian or academic spirit. As I have made clear in my previous works, I am a preacher; it can be no surprise, therefore, that in this book I have a pastoral and polemical intent. What is more, I intend to spell that purpose out.

Let me digress for a moment to say just a little more about this important matter. In quoting the following, I am not for a moment suggesting that my work can hold an academic candle to Alister McGrath's; I simply want to point up the contrast between my approach and that of the academic/publishing world. The publication of a book was proposed; McGrath explained the stance he and his publishers would adopt:

> I would write an introduction to Christian theology, not any specific form of Christian theology. The work would include discussion of Protestant, Catholic, Orthodox and Evangelical approaches to theology, treating all with respect and ensuring that they were properly represented; but it would not commend or adopt any of the specific views. It would be descriptive not prescriptive, allowing its users to understand what had been thought rather than telling them what to think. It would let them make up their own minds on core theological questions, rather than direct them to predetermined conclusions.[10]

Decidedly, that is not my approach. Indeed, McGrath and his publishers have offered a false dichotomy: in writing on spiritual matters, the choice is not either/or, but one of three. The alternatives are not simply 'descriptive': some say this, and others say that; you pays your money and takes your choice; and 'prescriptive': I am telling you what it is, and you have to believe it, especially since I am telling you what the favoured Confession (Westminster, 1689 or whatever) says. There is a third way – the scriptural way: this is what Scripture says – at least, as I see it – and you need to weigh it against Scripture in the spirit of Acts 17:11; the Berean Jews 'received the word

---

[10] Alister McGrath: *Through a Glass Darkly: Journeys through Science, Faith & Doubt – a Memoir*, Hodder & Stoughton, London, 2020, pp116-117.

[that is, the preaching of Paul and Silas] with all eagerness, examining the Scriptures daily to see if these things were so'.

This third way is my approach. If you find what I write contradicts Scripture, reject what I write; if, however, you find it is right according to Scripture – as you see Scripture, of course – then believe it. Moreover, we all need to turn the truth into action: 'If you know these things, blessed are you if you do them' (John 13:17). Christ did not close his great Sermon on the Mount[11] with the parable of the wise and foolish builders (Matt. 7:24-27) in order to provide material for Sunday-school teachers. Christ's encomium still stands: 'Blessed... are those who hear the word of God and keep it' (Luke 11:28). And James was clear enough: it is good to hear and know what Scripture says – no doubt about that! – but it is the doing of it that counts (Jas. 1:19-25; 2:8-9). A lecture informs; preaching informs us in order to make us feel in order to make us act. Mary, Christ's mother, spelled it out: 'Do whatever he tells you' (John 2:5).

And that is the spirit in which I write, that is the end I look for – in myself and others.

* * *

I am convinced that when it comes to thinking about the resurrection and the kingdom, most contemporary believers – and I include myself – are very different to the first believers, that we fall far short of them: Christ's resurrection and the kingdom do not play the vital role in our lives which they played in theirs. That being so, I have written this book in order to do what I can to help believers – and, once again, I include myself[12] – to recover what the first believers had in this regard; namely, the new-covenant attitude to Christ's resurrection and kingdom. Let me stress this: I am not writing in detail about the

---

[11] For more on this, see my *Smoke*.

[12] Writing on a subject always clarifies it for me. Trying to teach others, explaining to others, is a far better way to learn than listening to a monologue. Hence the value of mutual discussion over an open Bible (Heb. 10:24-25). See my *Sowed*; *Priesthood*.

resurrection and the kingdom. My concern is with the ways in which both resurrection and kingdom affected the life of the early *ekklēsia*, and contrasting that with the experience of many of us today.

Let me be specific. Take that which the Bible calls the believer's 'blessed hope', which will become a reality at 'the appearing of the glory of our great God and Saviour Jesus Christ' (Tit. 2:13). Sadly, most contemporary believers, by concentrating on the intermediate state – the immediate blessed condition after death of the believer in heaven with Christ – have effectively diminished this 'blessed hope'. They have reduced their own, personal resurrection at the second coming of Christ to a kind of tack-on, an after-thought, a postscript or epilogue, or even an interruption, a massive invasion, of the bliss already being enjoyed – leading to what? A more-or-less continuance of the same! Post-millennialism does something similar by encouraging believers to think about a flourishing earthly kingdom *before* Christ's return.

Christendom, which has deeply infected us all, must carry a large measure of responsibility for all this: as it has played havoc with so much else in the gospel, so it has done much to ruin (or, at least, severely reduce or diminish) the resurrection – in the first place, the resurrection of Christ – and, intimately associated with it, the resurrection of the believer.

Diminish the resurrection? Surely not! Let me justify my claim.

At best, for most believers today, the resurrection of Christ is something to think and sing about for an hour or so on a Christendom-designated[13] Sunday in early Spring. Forelocks can be pulled to it on 'ordinary' Sunday mornings, yes, but it really comes into its own on this high day in the Christendom

---

[13] In the seventh century, in order to settle a long-standing, heated quarrel about the date on which Easter should be observed, delegates at the Synod of Whitby devised a formula (in accordance with the Roman system) which is still used today – by most in Christendom, that is; the Orthodox and some Catholics opt for another day.

calendar – Easter Sunday. Truth to tell, the resurrection of Christ – and, therefore, their own resurrection – is of little practical consequence for most believers. Indeed, for many, a special church service, with officials and church furniture bedecked with flowers and material of selected colours, Easter eggs, Easter biscuits, Easter cards, furry bunnies and fluffy chicks, and all the rest of the Christendom paraphernalia, smother the bodily resurrection of Christ. Christendom rules OK![14]

The first believers, however, living as they did before Christendom had been invented, saw Christ's resurrection in a very different light. No chocolate cream-filled eggs or special biscuits for them! Christ's resurrection, to them, was the greatest event imaginable, towering above all else. They had come to see the resurrection as the fulfilment of long-awaited prophecy. Further, the resurrection was a solid, hard-nosed, hard-edged fact – now a doctrine – something to be preached, and preached by believers in their confrontation of the hostile cultures with which they were surrounded – Jewish, Greek and Roman – even though this would inevitably take them into ridicule, ostracism, pain and worse.

Let me correct myself. It wasn't so much that the first believers preached the doctrine of resurrection. I don't know as they ever did what so many Reformed men have done and still do – namely, preach doctrine (often, see above, delivered as a painstaking intellectual, formal lecture or essay): they preached the resurrected Christ, the resurrected Christ as King: 'What we proclaim is... Jesus Christ as Lord' (2 Cor. 4:5). That was what got them into trouble. Christ was not only lord; he was the Lord, the one and only Lord, the one to whom every knee would have to bow (Phil. 2:9-11).

---

[14] Christendom has not yet reduced the 'celebration' of Christ's resurrection to the same level of childishness and carnality as it has Christ's incarnation, but who knows if the two may not run neck and neck in the coming years? For more on Christendom, see Appendix 2 in my *Relationship*. See also my *Pastor*.

What is more, the resurrection of Christ, leading as it inevitably did to the assurance of their own resurrection, also served as a massive stimulus for them to live a life of holiness and gospel service. And, of course, as stated earlier, it was the foundation of their 'blessed hope'.[15] As Christ, just before his death, had declared:

> Yet a little while and the world will see me no more, but you will see me. Because I live, you also will live (John 14:19).

Let that sink in!

As John Calvin stated in his *Commentary* on the verse, believers are here taught to appreciate that 'the life of Christ is the cause of our life'. As Paul put it:

> If [that is, since] the Spirit of him who raised Jesus from the dead dwells in you, he who raised Christ Jesus from the dead will also give life to your mortal bodies through his Spirit who dwells in you (Rom. 8:11).[16]

Devastating stuff!

In short, the resurrection of Christ was of such importance to the first believers, that it is impossible to overstate its significance, its consequence in their lives. Paul expressed it in this way when writing to the believers in Corinth:

> God [who] raised the Lord and will also raise us up by his power (1 Cor. 6:14).

> If Christ has not been raised, your faith is futile and you are still in your sins. Then those also who have fallen asleep in Christ [that is, believers who have died] have perished. If in

---

[15] Recently, when preaching on John 8:56, I challenged us all with the fact that Abraham 'longed for the anticipated' day of Christ: do we, as believers, long for the appearance of the great God and our Saviour, Jesus Christ in his second coming? See the sermon 'Longing Anticipation' on my sermonaudio.com page.

[16] Some view this statement as a reference to progressive sanctification. The fact is, Christ's resurrection plays a key role in both the believer's progressive sanctification and his 'blessed hope'. See later.

Christ we have hope in this life only, we are of all people most to be pitied (1 Cor. 15:17-19).

The blunt truth is that if Christ has not been raised, the apostles were downright liars, their preaching was useless waffle, the believer's faith is pointless, utterly misguided, based on a glaring fabrication, and the believer is still a slave of sin and ruined by it; moreover, he is left without a glimmer of hope; when he dies he snuffs it, worms feed on him (Job 19:26), and he moulders to dust in the ground – as Christ himself did! And that's the end of it!

The New Testament never tires of making the point; it constantly puts all its eggs in the one basket; all or nothing: if Christ is not raised, no believer is saved (Rom. 10:9), no believer is justified (Rom. 4:25), no believer has new life (Rom. 6:4), no believer is united to Christ (Rom. 7:4), no believer spiritually seated with Christ in glory even now (Eph. 2:6), no believer will himself be reunited with his body when it is raised from the dead (2 Cor. 4:14), no believer is or will be delivered from God's wrath (1 Thess. 1:10), but his trust is in a gospel which is a lie (2 Tim. 2:8), and every believer is wasting his existence depending on a delusion (1 Pet. 1:21). And so on.

The first believers saw all that, and more; no wonder, then, that the resurrection was of prime importance to them. The question is, does the resurrection *consciously* play such a role in our lives?

There is another issue – somewhat more nuanced. Most believers – and, yet again, I include myself – when they do try to think deeply about the resurrection, draw conclusions which are far too limited. There is more to Christ's resurrection than victory over death, for instance. It is that, of course. But that is not enough to account for the new-covenant emphasis on the resurrection. Nor should Christ's resurrection be limited to vindicating his work on the cross. It certainly did that! Again, it clearly and publicly showed that the Father was well-pleased – fully satisfied – with his Son's life and sacrifice, and that his wrath towards his elect had been completely and utterly propitiated by his Son's sufferings. Yes, indeed. And, of course, it is gloriously true, as Paul so powerfully concluded his argument on Abraham's faith, by saying that the patriarch's:

> ...faith was 'counted to him as righteousness'. But the words 'it was counted to him' were not written for his sake alone, but for ours also. It will be counted to us who believe in him who raised from the dead Jesus our Lord, who was delivered up for our trespasses and raised for our justification (Rom. 4:22-25).[17]

But – and here comes the nuance I referred to – even all this (right though it is) does not exhaust the doctrine of the resurrection of Christ.

This is the point. I am afraid that many believers have reduced the resurrection and lost immensely by it. They have thought of

---

[17] But many limit the 'raised for our justification' as to mean 'raised in order to authenticate the fact that he had wrought our justification on the cross'. I am convinced this is a mistake. I quote from my *Imputed*: 'Paul used *dia* twice: "delivered up for (*dia*) our trespasses and raised for (*dia*) our justification". The same weight, surely, must be given in each case. In my view, it is far too weak to say that Christ was raised from the dead simply to vindicate his work, or give proof of the justification he had accomplished for his people on the cross, or to demonstrate that God was being fair to Christ in that since he had earned the pardon, so it was only right that he should be raised. The apostle used *dia*, "for", "on account of", in both parts of the sentence. Christ was delivered up *dia* our offences, and was raised *dia* our justification. The apostle clearly attributes the same weight and power to the resurrection as he does to the death of Christ as far as justification goes. Writing to believers, Paul could say that Christ died for our sins, on account of our sins, to deal with our sins, in order to deliver us from our offences, and likewise he was raised for our justification, on account of our justification, in order to justify us. This passage, I suggest, on its own, drives a coach and horses through the passive-obedience-only view. "Vindication" for the second *dia* is woefully inadequate. The truth is, union with Christ is the key to this entire discussion, and union with Christ involves union with him in his death *and* resurrection (Rom. 6:4-8)'. See my *Imputed* for my argument show that Christ's life of active obedience to the law plays a vital role in the believer's justification: that justification is not confined to Christ's passive obedience – his death on the cross.

it in somewhat negative terms; the time has long passed for them to wake up to the positive. In this work I want to do something to encourage that shift.

No doubt some will be thinking that I am, yet again, up to my old tricks and overstating the case. If so, perhaps a contemporary illustration might help some to re-think. We have all met – and probably used – the phrase 'from the cradle to grave'. Many believers talk, think – and not a few preach and write – in such terms. Take Tim Keller, in a recent book:

> Life is a journey, and finding and knowing God is fundamental to that journey. When a new child is born, when we approach marriage, and when we find ourselves facing death – either in old age or much earlier – it tends to concentrate the mind... The most fundamental transition any human being can make is what the Bible refers to as the new birth (John 3:1-8), or becoming a 'new creation' (2 Cor.5:17)... We [Keller and his wife] want to help readers facing major life changes to think about what constitutes the truly changed life... We start with birth..., move into marriage, and conclude with death.[18]

I am not nitpicking when I say that although, of course, there is truth in this, it is far from the whole truth. Death is not the end – no, not for any man, believer or unbeliever. Far from it! In this work, I am primarily concerned with the believer. Death is certainly not the end for the believer. *But nor is the intermediate state.* The end for the believer is the return of Christ, which will bring about the believer's own resurrection to be forever with Christ and the enjoyment of eternal bliss. And all this is guaranteed and accomplished by the resurrection of Christ himself.

Scripturally speaking, there are two fixed points for the believer. The first is his election to everlasting salvation in God's decree

---

[18] Opening in Timothy Keller: *On Death*, Hodder & Stoughton, London, 2020. I have omitted his reference to infant sprinkling because the rite is totally unscriptural and, alas, has had dire eternal consequences for untold millions.

in eternity past. Here is a sample of scriptural extracts which declare it:

As many as were appointed to eternal life believed (Acts 13:48).

We know that for those who love God all things work together for good, for those who are called according to his purpose. For those whom he foreknew he also predestined to be conformed to the image of his Son, in order that he might be the firstborn among many brothers. And those whom he predestined he also called, and those whom he called he also justified, and those whom he justified he also glorified (Rom. 8:28-30).

[The Father] chose us in [Christ] before the foundation of the world, that we should be holy and blameless before him. In love he predestined us for adoption as sons through Jesus Christ, according to the purpose of his will... (Eph. 1:4-5).

We ought always to give thanks to God for you, brothers beloved by the Lord, because God chose you as the firstfruits to be saved, through sanctification by the Spirit and belief in the truth (2 Thess. 2:13).

[God] saved us and called us to a holy calling, not because of our works but because of his own purpose and grace, which he gave us in Christ Jesus before the ages began (2 Tim. 1:9).

To those who are elect... according to the foreknowledge of God the Father, in the sanctification of the Spirit, for obedience to Jesus Christ and for sprinkling with his blood (2 Pet. 1:1-2).

Of his own [eternal] will [the Father] brought us forth by the word of truth, that we should be a kind of firstfruits of his creatures (Jas. 1:18).

The second fixed point for the believer is not his death; nor is it the intermediate state. Rather, it is his everlasting bliss in the new heavens and the new earth in the eternal kingdom of Christ which will be fully established after the general resurrection of all the dead, followed by the final judgment, at Christ's return.[19] I supply no passages at this point to prove it; that is one of the main purposes of the rest of the book.

---

[19] The final fixed point for the unbeliever is eternal damnation.

* * *

In order to try to break through the stubborn crust of centuries of
Christendom to get back to the days of the first believers – those
men and women who were deeply conscious that Christ had
risen – I intend to be fulsome in quoting Scripture. It is all we
have; it is all we need. What is more, when they apply to various
aspects of what I want to say, some extracts will be repeated. I
make no apology for this. It shows the air the first believers
breathed, the atmosphere in which they lived and died. It shows
us what we have lost and what we must regain.

Just think: What argument could an early believer use to
convince a pagan that Christ was truly God, truly King? His
lowly birth? The way his parents were forced to carry him as a
babe in arms while fleeing as refugees to Egypt to escape the
child's slaughter under Herod? His hidden life in a carpenter's
shed in an obscure village, miles from any place of importance?
And when he did go public, his rejection by the bulk of Jews,
not least the Jewish leaders, the theologians, the politicians of
clout? What about his betrayal and desertion? His tragic trial?
His ignominious death? Burial? Would the rehearsal this –
however polished the lecture, however professionally illustrated
the PowerPoint – have convinced any Jew, any Roman (who,
inevitably, thought in terms of military and political power), any
Greek (who, inevitably, thought in terms of philosophy), or any
other pagan (like the Romans and Greeks, soaked in a
multiplicity of gods, governed by the occult and witchcraft)?
Surely not! It must have been – it could only have been – the
passionate and effective preaching of Christ in his resurrection.
Yes, his miraculous powers, of course – but what greater
miracle than his resurrection? And in the ultimate? His return as
Judge – the King bringing in his kingdom in all its glory.

The recovery of that is what I write for: may my little book
contribute to it.

Making the Point

Scripture forges an unbreakable link between Christ's resurrection, his kingship and kingdom, his coming again and the resurrection of all men (especially, for my purposes, the resurrection of believers), and the eternal consequences of all of that. Moreover, Scripture shows us that all these issues played a major role in the life of the early *ekklēsia*. The weight the apostles gave to these questions as they, in accordance with Christ's promise (John 14:26; 16:12-15,25), wrote Scripture for the *ekklēsia* in the opening years of the new covenant, leaves us with no other conclusion.

Where to start?

Consider what must surely be the principal passage. Paul knew that some believers in Corinth had strayed into error over the resurrection; some were even denying its very existence. This rightly filled the apostle with alarm. Consequently, before he signed off his first letter to Corinth, he devoted a considerable amount of time to dealing with all the ramifications of resurrection, and so leaving on record the classic doctrinal statement on the subject:

> Now I would remind you, brothers, of the gospel I preached to you, which you received, in which you stand, and by which you are being saved, if you hold fast to the word I preached to you – unless you believed in vain. For I delivered to you as of first importance what I also received: that Christ died for our sins in accordance with the Scriptures, that he was buried, that he was raised on the third day in accordance with the Scriptures... So we preach and so you believed.
> Now if Christ is proclaimed as raised from the dead, how can some of you say that there is no resurrection of the dead? But if there is no resurrection of the dead, then not even Christ has been raised. And if Christ has not been raised, then our preaching is in vain and your faith is in vain. We are even found to be misrepresenting God, because we testified about God that he raised Christ, whom he did not raise if it is true that the dead are not raised. For if the dead are not raised, not

even Christ has been raised. And if Christ has not been raised, your faith is futile and you are still in your sins. Then those also who have fallen asleep in Christ have perished. If in Christ we have hope in this life only, we are of all people most to be pitied.

Paul has stated it bluntly: no resurrection, nothing! 'But', he thundered, using one of the most glorious words of the new covenant, 'but in fact...':

But in fact Christ has been raised from the dead, the firstfruits of those who have fallen asleep. For as by a man came death, by a man has come also the resurrection of the dead. For as in Adam all die, so also in Christ shall all be made alive. But each in his own order: Christ the firstfruits, then at his coming those who belong to Christ. Then comes the end, when he delivers the kingdom to God the Father after destroying every rule and every authority and power. For he must reign until he has put all his enemies under his feet. The last enemy to be destroyed is death...

Otherwise, what do people mean by being baptised on behalf of the dead? If the dead are not raised at all, why are people baptised on their behalf? Why are we in danger every hour? I protest, brothers, by my pride in you, which I have in Christ Jesus our Lord, I die every day! What do I gain if, humanly speaking, I fought with beasts at Ephesus? If the dead are not raised: 'Let us eat and drink, for tomorrow we die'...

...the resurrection of the dead... What is sown is perishable; what is raised is imperishable. It is sown in dishonour; it is raised in glory. It is sown in weakness; it is raised in power. It is sown a natural body; it is raised a spiritual body. If there is a natural body, there is also a spiritual body. Thus it is written: 'The first man Adam became a living being', the last Adam became a life-giving spirit. But it is not the spiritual that is first but the natural, and then the spiritual. The first man was from the earth, a man of dust; the second man is from heaven. As was the man of dust, so also are those who are of the dust, and as is the man of heaven, so also are those who are of heaven. Just as we have borne the image of the man of dust, we shall also bear the image of the man of heaven.

I tell you this, brothers: flesh and blood cannot inherit the kingdom of God, nor does the perishable inherit the imperishable. Behold! I tell you a mystery. We shall not all sleep, but we shall all be changed, in a moment, in the twinkling of an eye, at the last trumpet. For the trumpet will sound, and the dead will be raised imperishable, and we shall be changed. For this perishable body must put on the imperishable, and this mortal body must put on immortality. When the perishable puts on the imperishable, and the mortal puts on immortality, then shall come to pass the saying that is written: 'Death is swallowed up in victory. O death, where is your victory? O death, where is your sting?'

The sting of death is sin, and the power of sin is the law. But thanks be to God, who gives us the victory through our Lord Jesus Christ.

Therefore, my beloved brothers, be steadfast, immovable, always abounding in the work of the Lord, knowing that in the Lord your labour is not in vain (1 Cor. 15:1-58).

I have quoted this passage at length to let Paul's majestic statement speak for itself. And how it does speak! Speak? It shouts its meaning from the rooftop. Paul was writing to believers. What is the believer's hope, the believer's comfort in suffering, his courage in persecution, his stimulus to holiness of life and effort in gospel labour, his consolation at the graveside of a fellow-believer and in facing his own death? It is Christ's resurrection, and hence the believer's own resurrection into the full experience of Christ's kingdom with all the saints at the last day. The last day! So important is this scriptural phrase, let me put it in capitals: the Last Day.

'The Last Day', 'the Day of the Lord', and the like – what 'Day' is this? Now it is true that the Old Testament is full of references (both explicit and implicit) which bear on this 'Day', but (as I have already noted and will explore more fully), since the first disciples needed to be taught to re-think their understanding of such references, and, consequently, their Messianic/kingdom expectations, we must let the New Testament (the new covenant) tell us what we are to understand by 'the Day'.[1] As it does, time and again. But just before I demonstrate the point, let

---

[1] How long the list would be if I included the Old Testament references! As for Old Testament passages bearing on God's kingdom, see, for instance, Ex. 15:18; Ps. 10:16; 29:10; 68:1-35; 146:10; Jer. 10:10; Lam. 5:19; Dan. 2:44; 4:34; 6:26; 7:27.

us remind ourselves that the prophets had warned Israel that the coming Day – the Day they longed for – would be very different to their expectations:

> Woe to you who desire *the day of the LORD*! Why would you have *the day of the LORD*? It is darkness, and not light, as if a man fled from a lion, and a bear met him, or went into the house and leaned his hand against the wall, and a serpent bit him. Is not *the day of the LORD* darkness, and not light, and gloom with no brightness in it? I hate, I despise your feasts, and I take no delight in your solemn assemblies. Even though you offer me your burnt offerings and grain offerings, I will not accept them; and the peace offerings of your fattened animals, I will not look upon them. Take away from me the noise of your songs; to the melody of your harps I will not listen. But let justice roll down like waters, and righteousness like an ever-flowing stream (Amos 5:18-24).

> Behold, I send my messenger, and he will prepare the way before me. And the Lord whom you seek will suddenly come to his temple; and the messenger of the covenant in whom you delight, behold, he is coming, says the LORD of hosts. But who can endure *the day of his coming*, and who can stand when he appears? For he is like a refiner's fire and like fullers' soap (Mal. 3:1-2).

On the basis of such prophecies, the Jews of Christ's day should have tempered their triumphalist expectations. Alas, as we know, they did not.

And now for the New Testament:

> Concerning *that day* and hour no one knows, not even the angels of heaven, nor the Son, but the Father only (Matt. 24:36).

> As the lightning flashes and lights up the sky from one side to the other, so will the Son of Man be in his *day*. But first he must suffer many things and be rejected by this generation. Just as it was in the days of Noah, so will it be in *the days of the Son of Man*. They were eating and drinking and marrying and being given in marriage, until the day when Noah entered the ark, and the flood came and destroyed them all. Likewise, just as it was in the days of Lot – they were eating and drinking, buying and selling, planting and building, but on the day when

Lot went out from Sodom, fire and sulphur rained from heaven and destroyed them all – so will it be on *the day when the Son of Man is revealed* (Luke 17:24-30).

Watch yourselves lest your hearts be weighed down with dissipation and drunkenness and cares of this life, and *that day* come upon you suddenly like a trap (Luke 21:34).

And this is the will of him who sent me, that I should lose nothing of all that he has given me, but raise it up on *the last day*. For this is the will of my Father, that everyone who looks on the Son and believes in him should have eternal life, and I will raise him up on *the last day* (John 6:39-40).

I will show wonders in the heavens above and signs on the earth below, blood, and fire, and vapour of smoke; the sun shall be turned to darkness and the moon to blood, before *the day of the Lord* comes, *the great and magnificent day* (Acts 2:19-20; see Joel 2:28-32).

Because of your hard and impenitent heart you are storing up wrath for yourself on *the day of wrath* when God's righteous *judgment* will be revealed... on *that da*y when, according to my gospel, God judges the secrets of men by Christ Jesus (Rom. 2:5,16).

Each one's work will become manifest, for *the day* will disclose it, because it will be revealed by fire, and the fire will test what sort of work each one has done (1 Cor. 3:13).

When you are assembled in the name of the Lord Jesus and my spirit is present, with the power of our Lord Jesus, you are to deliver this man to Satan for the destruction of the flesh, so that his spirit may be saved in *the day of the Lord* (1 Cor. 5:5).

We are not writing to you anything other than what you read and understand and I hope you will fully understand... that on *the day of our Lord Jesus* you will boast of us as we will boast of you (2 Cor. 1:13-14).

Do not grieve the Holy Spirit of God, by whom you were sealed for *the day of redemption* (Eph. 4:30).

I am sure of this, that he who began a good work in you will bring it to completion at *the day of Jesus Christ* (Phil. 1:6).

It is my prayer that your love may abound more and more, with knowledge and all discernment, so that you may approve what is excellent, and so be pure and blameless for *the day of Christ* (Phil. 1:9-10).

Do all things without grumbling or disputing, that you may be blameless and innocent, children of God without blemish in the midst of a crooked and twisted generation, among whom you shine as lights in the world, holding fast to the word of life, so that in *the day of Christ* I may be proud that I did not run in vain or labour in vain (Phil. 2:14-19).

You yourselves are fully aware that *the day of the Lord* will come like a thief in the night... But you are not in darkness, brothers, for *that day* to surprise you like a thief (1 Thess. 5:2-4).

Now concerning the coming of our Lord Jesus Christ and our being gathered together to him, we ask you, brothers, not to be quickly shaken in mind or alarmed, either by a spirit or a spoken word, or a letter seeming to be from us, to the effect that *the day of the Lord* has come. Let no one deceive you in any way. For *that day* will not come, unless the rebellion comes first, and the man of lawlessness is revealed (2 Thess. 2:1-12).

Christ Jesus... abolished death and brought life and immortality to light through the gospel, for which I was appointed a preacher and apostle and teacher, which is why I suffer as I do. But I am not ashamed, for I know whom I have believed, and I am convinced that he is able to guard until *that day* what has been entrusted to me (2 Tim. 1:10-12).

There is laid up for me the crown of righteousness, which the Lord, the righteous judge, will award to me on *that day*, and not only to me but also to all who have loved his appearing (2 Tim. 4:8).

Let us consider how to stir up one another to love and good works, not neglecting to meet together, as is the habit of some, but encouraging one another, and all the more as you see *the day* drawing near (Heb. 10:24-25).

Blessed be the God and Father of our Lord Jesus Christ! According to his great mercy, he has caused us to be born again to a living hope through the resurrection of Jesus Christ from the dead, to an inheritance that is imperishable, undefiled, and unfading, kept in heaven for you, who by God's power are being guarded through faith for a salvation ready to be revealed in *the last time*. In this you rejoice, though now for a little while, if necessary, you have been grieved by various trials, so that the tested genuineness of your faith – more precious than gold that perishes though it is tested by fire – may be found to result in praise and glory and honour at *the revelation of Jesus Christ*. Though you have not seen him, you love him. Though you do not now see him, you believe in him and rejoice with joy that is inexpressible and filled with glory, obtaining the outcome of your faith, the salvation of your souls (1 Pet. 1:3-9).

Set your hope fully on the grace that will be brought to you at *the revelation of Jesus Christ* (1 Pet. 1:13).

Rejoice insofar as you share Christ's sufferings, that you may also rejoice and be glad *when his glory is revealed* (1 Pet. 4:13).

I exhort the elders among you, as a fellow elder and a witness of the sufferings of Christ, as well as a partaker in *the glory that is going to be revealed*... And *when the chief Shepherd appears*, you will receive the unfading crown of glory (1 Pet. 5:1,4).

God did not spare angels when they sinned, but cast them into hell and committed them to chains of gloomy darkness to be kept until the *judgment*... The Lord knows how to rescue the godly from trials, and to keep the unrighteous under punishment until *the day of judgment* (2 Pet. 2:4,9).

The heavens and earth that now exist are stored up for fire, being kept until *the day of judgment and destruction of the ungodly*... The Lord is not slow to fulfil his promise as some count slowness, but is patient toward you, not wishing that any should perish, but that all should reach repentance. But *the day of the Lord* will come like a thief, and then the heavens will pass away with a roar, and the heavenly bodies will be burned up and dissolved, and the earth and the works that are done on it will be exposed. Since all these things are thus to be dissolved, what sort of people ought you to be in lives of holiness and godliness, waiting for and hastening the coming of *the day of God*, because of which the heavens will be set on fire and dissolved, and the heavenly bodies will melt as they burn! But according to his promise we are waiting for new heavens and a new earth in which righteousness dwells. Therefore, beloved, since you are waiting for these, be diligent to be found by him without spot or blemish, and at peace. And count the patience of our Lord as salvation... You therefore, beloved, knowing this beforehand, take care that you are not carried away with the error of lawless people and lose your own stability. But grow in the grace and knowledge of our Lord and Saviour Jesus Christ. To him be the glory both now and to the ***day*** of eternity. Amen (2 Pet. 3:7-18).

And now, little children, abide in him, so that ***when he appears*** we may have confidence and not shrink from him in shame at his coming (1 John 2:28).

Beloved, we are God's children now, and what we will be has not yet appeared; but we know that ***when he appears*** we shall be like him, because we shall see him as he is. And everyone who thus hopes in him purifies himself as he is pure (1 John 3:2-3).

By this we know that we abide in him and he in us, because he has given us of his Spirit. And we have seen and testify that the Father has sent his Son to be the Saviour of the world. Whoever confesses that Jesus is the Son of God, God abides in him, and he in God. So we have come to know and to believe the love that God has for us. God is love, and whoever abides in love abides in God, and God abides in him. By this is love perfected with us, so that we may have confidence for ***the day of judgment***, because as he is so also are we in this world (1 John 4:13-17).

The angels who did not stay within their own position of authority, but left their proper dwelling, he has kept in eternal chains under gloomy darkness until ***the judgment of the great day*** (Jude 6).

Have I overwhelmed you by this weight of quotation? I offer no apology. As I said in the Introduction, I want to set out as clearly as I can the amount of space – the weight – the New Testament gives (both explicitly and implicitly) to the resurrection and the kingdom. As these extracts show, not only in their addresses to unbelievers, but especially when speaking or writing to believers in order to encourage, comfort, challenge, exhort, urge, command, rebuke or stir them, the apostles were unstinted in their references to the coming Day, the last Day, the Day of Christ. Clearly, the thought of the day of Christ's return, that Day which will usher in the resurrection of all men, then their judgment, followed by their entrance either into the eternal glory of the kingdom or into eternal damnation, played a massive role in the life of the early *ekklēsia*. And not only as something to be preserved within the confines of the *ekklēsia*: since all men will be raised and face judgment, the coming Day figured prominently in the *ekklēsia's* attitude and approach to outsiders.

Let me underline the material point: death is not the end, but there is a coming Day – Christ's Day – when all men will be raised, either to eternal glory or eternal damnation, and this is only possible because Christ himself was raised from the dead.

In order to emphasise the vital connection between all these issues, here are some more extracts (I include some of the extracts already quoted in order to preserve the full sense of the scriptural argument). I start with a couple from the Old Testament:

> I know that my Redeemer lives, and at the last he will stand upon the earth. And after my skin has been thus destroyed, yet in my flesh I shall see God, whom I shall see for myself, and my eyes shall behold, and not another. My heart faints within me! (Job 19:25-27).

> My heart is glad, and my whole being rejoices; my flesh also dwells secure. For you will not abandon my soul to Sheol, or let your holy one see corruption (Ps. 16:9-10).

And now for the New:

> As the lightning flashes and lights up the sky from one side to the other, so will the Son of Man be in his day. But first he must suffer many things and be rejected by this generation. Just as it was in the days of Noah, so will it be in the days of the Son of Man. They were eating and drinking and marrying and being given in marriage, until the day when Noah entered the ark, and the flood came and destroyed them all. Likewise, just

as it was in the days of Lot – they were eating and drinking, buying and selling, planting and building, but on the day when Lot went out from Sodom, fire and sulphur rained from heaven and destroyed them all – so will it be on the day when the Son of Man is revealed (Luke 17:24-30).

The powers of the heavens will be shaken. And then they will see the Son of Man coming in a cloud with power and great glory. Now when these things begin to take place, straighten up and raise your heads, because your redemption is drawing near... When you see these things taking place, you know that the kingdom of God is near (Luke 21:26-28,31).

Truly, truly, I say to you, an hour is coming, and is now here, when the dead will hear the voice of the Son of God, and those who hear will live. For as the Father has life in himself, so he has granted the Son also to have life in himself. And he has given him authority to execute judgment, because he is the Son of Man. Do not marvel at this, for an hour is coming when all who are in the tombs will hear his voice and come out, those who have done good to the resurrection of life, and those who have done evil to the resurrection of judgment (John 5:25-29).

In my Father's house are many rooms. If it were not so, would I have told you that I go to prepare a place for you? And if I go and prepare a place for you, I will come again and will take you to myself, that where I am you may be also (John 14:2-3).

I will show wonders in the heavens above and signs on the earth below, blood, and fire, and vapour of smoke; the sun shall be turned to darkness and the moon to blood, before the day of the Lord comes, the great and magnificent day (Acts 2:19-20; see Joel 2:28-32).

My brothers, you also have died to the law through the body of Christ, so that you may belong to another, to him who has been raised from the dead, in order that we may bear fruit for God (Rom. 7:4).

[Since] the Spirit of him who raised Jesus from the dead dwells in you, he who raised Christ Jesus from the dead will also give life to your mortal bodies through his Spirit who dwells in you (Rom. 8:11).

We... who have the firstfruits of the Spirit, groan inwardly as we wait eagerly for adoption as sons, the redemption of our bodies. For in this hope we were saved. Now hope that is seen is not hope. For who hopes for what he sees? But if we hope for what we do not see, we wait for it with patience (Rom. 8:23-25).

Who shall bring any charge against God's elect? It is God who justifies. Who is to condemn? Christ Jesus is the one who died – more than that, who was raised – who is at the right hand of God, who indeed is interceding for us (Rom. 8:33-34).

If you confess with your mouth that Jesus is Lord and believe in your heart that God raised him from the dead, you will be saved (Rom. 10:9).

You wait for the revealing of our Lord Jesus Christ, who will sustain you to the end, guiltless in the day of our Lord Jesus Christ (1 Cor. 1:7-8).

When you are assembled in the name of the Lord Jesus and my spirit is present, with the power of our Lord Jesus, you are to deliver this man to Satan for the destruction of the flesh, so that his spirit may be saved in the day of the Lord (1 Cor. 5:5).

God raised the Lord (1 Cor. 6:14).

We are not writing to you anything other than what you read and understand and I hope you will fully understand... that on the day of our Lord Jesus you will boast of us as we will boast of you (2 Cor. 1:13-14).

We were so utterly burdened beyond our strength that we despaired of life itself. Indeed, we felt that we had received the sentence of death. But that was to make us rely not on ourselves but on God who raises the dead (2 Cor. 1:8-9).

He who raised the Lord Jesus will raise us also with Jesus and bring us with you into his presence (2 Cor. 4:14).

Paul, an apostle... through Jesus Christ and God the Father, who raised him from the dead (Gal. 1:1).

In [Christ]... when you heard the word of truth, the gospel of your salvation, and believed in him, [you] were sealed with the promised Holy Spirit, who is the guarantee of our inheritance until we acquire possession of it [that is, until God redeems his possession], to the praise of his glory (Eph. 1:13-14).

God, being rich in mercy, because of the great love with which he loved us, even when we were dead in our trespasses, made us alive together with Christ – by grace you have been saved – and raised us up with him and seated us with him in the heavenly places in Christ Jesus, so that in the coming ages he might show the immeasurable riches of his grace in kindness toward us in Christ Jesus (Eph. 2:4-7).

Do not grieve the Holy Spirit of God, by whom you were sealed for the day of redemption (Eph. 4:30).

I am sure of this, that he who began a good work in you will bring it to completion at the day of Jesus Christ (Phil. 1:6).

It is my prayer that your love may abound more and more, with knowledge and all discernment, so that you may approve what is excellent, and so be pure and blameless for the day of Christ (Phil. 1:9-10).

God has highly exalted [Christ] and bestowed on him the name that is above every name, so that at the name of Jesus every knee should bow, in heaven and on earth and under the earth, and every tongue confess that Jesus Christ is Lord, to the glory of God the Father (Phil. 2:9-11).

Do all things without grumbling or disputing, that you may be blameless and innocent, children of God without blemish in the midst of a crooked and twisted generation, among whom you shine as lights in the world, holding fast to the word of life, so that in the day of Christ I may be proud that I did not run in vain or labour in vain (Phil. 2:14-19).

...that I may know him and the power of his resurrection, and may share his sufferings, becoming like him in his death, that by any means possible I may attain the resurrection from the dead (Phil. 3:10-11).

Our citizenship is in heaven, and from it we await a Saviour, the Lord Jesus Christ, who will transform our lowly body to be like his glorious body, by the power that enables him even to subject all things to himself (Phil. 3:20-21).

God... raised him from the dead (Col. 2:12).

If [since] then you have been raised with Christ, seek the things that are above, where Christ is, seated at the right hand of God. Set your minds on things that are above, not on things that are on earth. For you have died, and your life is hidden with Christ in God. When Christ who is your life appears, then you also will appear with him in glory (Col. 3:1-4).

You turned to God from idols to serve the living and true God, and to wait for his Son from heaven, whom he raised from the dead, Jesus who delivers us from the wrath to come (1 Thess. 1:9-10).

What is our hope or joy or crown of boasting before our Lord Jesus at his coming? Is it not you? For you are our glory and joy (1 Thess. 2:19-20).

May the Lord make you increase and abound in love for one another and for all, as we do for you, so that he may establish your hearts blameless in holiness before our God and Father, at the coming of our Lord Jesus with all his saints (1 Thess. 3:12-13).

You yourselves are fully aware that the day of the Lord will come like a thief in the night (1 Thess. 5:2).

Now concerning the coming of our Lord Jesus Christ and our being gathered together to him, we ask you, brothers, not to be quickly shaken in mind or alarmed, either by a spirit or a spoken word, or a letter seeming to be from us, to the effect that the day of the Lord has come. Let no one deceive you in any way. For that day will not come, unless the rebellion comes first, and the man of lawlessness is revealed... (2 Thess. 2:1-12).

Christ Jesus... abolished death and brought life and immortality to light through the gospel, for which I was appointed a preacher and apostle and teacher, which is why I suffer as I do. But I am not ashamed, for I know whom I have believed, and I am convinced that he is able to guard until that day what has been entrusted to me (2 Tim. 1:10-12).

Remember Jesus Christ, risen from the dead, the offspring of David, as preached in my gospel... If we endure, we will also reign with him (2 Tim. 2:8,12).

I charge you in the presence of God and of Christ Jesus, who is to judge the living and the dead, and by his appearing and his kingdom: preach the word... (1 Tim. 4:1-2).

There is laid up for me the crown of righteousness, which the Lord, the righteous judge, will award to me on that day, and not only to me but also to all who have loved his appearing (2 Tim. 4:8).

The Lord will rescue me from every evil deed and bring me safely into his heavenly kingdom. To him be the glory forever and ever. Amen (1 Tim. 4:18).

[As believers, we are] waiting for our blessed hope, the appearing of the glory of our great God and Saviour Jesus Christ (Tit. 2:13).

[Abraham, the father of the faithful] was looking forward to the city that has foundations, whose designer and builder is God... [Believers] desire a better country, that is, a heavenly one. Therefore God is not ashamed to be called their God, for he has prepared for them a city... Let us be grateful for receiving a kingdom that cannot be shaken... Here we have no lasting city, but we seek the city that is to come (Heb. 11:10,16; 12:28; 13:14).

Blessed be the God and Father of our Lord Jesus Christ! According to his great mercy, he has caused us to be born again to a living hope through the resurrection of Jesus Christ from the dead, to an inheritance that is imperishable, undefiled, and unfading, kept in heaven for you, who by God's power are being guarded through faith for a salvation ready to be revealed in the last time. In this you rejoice, though now for a little while, if necessary, you have been grieved by various trials, so that the tested genuineness of your faith – more precious than gold that perishes though it is tested by fire – may be found to result in praise and glory and honour at the revelation of Jesus Christ. Though you have not seen him, you love him. Though you do not now see him, you believe in him and rejoice with joy that is inexpressible and filled with glory, obtaining the outcome of your faith, the salvation of your souls (1 Pet. 1:3-9).

Set your hope fully on the grace that will be brought to you at the revelation of Jesus Christ... God...raised him from the dead and gave him glory, so that your faith and hope are in God (1 Pet. 1:13,21).

Christ also suffered once for sins, the righteous for the unrighteous, that he might bring us to God, being put to death in the flesh but made alive in the spirit [or 'in spirit'; or 'in the Spirit'] (1 Pet. 3:18).

Rejoice insofar as you share Christ's sufferings, that you may also rejoice and be glad when his glory is revealed (1 Pet. 4:13).

When the chief Shepherd appears, you will receive the unfading crown of glory (1 Pet. 5:4).

I exhort the elders among you, as a fellow elder and a witness of the sufferings of Christ, as well as a partaker in the glory that is going to be revealed (1 Pet. 5:1).

The heavens and earth that now exist are stored up for fire, being kept until the day of judgment and destruction of the ungodly... The Lord is not slow to fulfil his promise as some count slowness, but is patient toward you, not wishing that any should perish, but that all should reach repentance. But the day of the Lord will come like a thief, and then the heavens will pass away with a roar, and the heavenly bodies will be burned up and dissolved, and the earth and the works that are done on it will be exposed. Since all these things are thus to be dissolved, what sort of people ought you to be in lives of holiness and godliness, waiting for and hastening the coming of the day of God, because of which the heavens will be set on fire and dissolved, and the heavenly bodies will melt as they burn! But according to his promise we are waiting for new heavens and a new earth in which righteousness dwells. Therefore, beloved, since you are waiting for these, be diligent to be found by him without spot or blemish, and at peace. And count the patience of our Lord as salvation (2 Pet. 3:7-15).

Beloved, we are God's children now, and what we will be has not yet appeared; but we know that when he appears we shall be like him, because we shall see him as he is. And everyone who thus hopes in him purifies himself as he is pure (1 John 3:2-3).

And let us never forget (alas, how often we do!) that Christ's return is a note to be sounded (and in no muted or formal way, or as a mere tack-on!) at the Lord's supper:

For as often as you eat this bread and drink the cup, you proclaim the Lord's death until he comes (1 Cor. 11:26).

Of course, at the supper we look back – back to the cross – but every time we break bread we remind ourselves – we are to be reminded – that Christ will return and bring in his kingdom:

> Now as they were eating, Jesus took bread, and after blessing it broke it and gave it to the disciples, and said: 'Take, eat; this is my body'. And he took a cup, and when he had given thanks he gave it to them, saying: 'Drink of it, all of you, for this is my blood of the new covenant, which is poured out for many for the forgiveness of sins. I tell you I will not drink again of this fruit of the vine until that day when I drink it new with you in my Father's kingdom' (Matt. 26:26-29; see also Luke 22:16,29-30).

And what a promise at the supper:

> I assign to you, as my Father assigned to me, a kingdom, that you may eat and drink at my table in my kingdom and sit on thrones judging the twelve tribes of Israel (Luke 22:29-30).

As these many extracts show – I said I would be unstinted in my quotation of Scripture – the apostles, and thus first believers in general, made much of the resurrection of Christ, his return, and the resurrection of all men. In particular, they made much of their own resurrection (because of the resurrection of Christ, himself the firstfruits or pledge), and their subsequent, certain entrance into the full glories of the kingdom.

The kingdom? Yes, indeed, with Christ as King of that kingdom.

From start to finish in Christ's life on earth, the message the Gospel writers convey is the same: from his birth, through death to his resurrection, Jesus always was and always is the expected (as promised by the prophets) Messiah, the Anointed, the King, the Son of God. Let me highlight the appropriate words in Luke's account of the birth of Christ, and Matthew's account of the crucifixion:

> [The angel, addressing Mary, told her:] 'You will conceive in your womb and bear a son, and you shall call his name Jesus. He will be great and will be called *the Son of the Most High*. And the Lord God will give to him *the throne of his father*

David, and ***he will reign over the house of Jacob forever***, and
of ***his kingdom*** there will be no end... The Holy Spirit will
come upon you, and the power of the Most High will
overshadow you; therefore the child to be born will be called
holy – ***the Son of God***'...

[Elizabeth addressed Mary as] 'the mother of my ***Lord***'...

[Zechariah declared:] 'Blessed be the Lord God of Israel, for
he has visited and redeemed his people and has raised up ***a
horn of salvation*** for us in the house of his servant David, as
he spoke by the mouth of his holy prophets from of old, that we
should be saved from our enemies and from the hand of all
who hate us; to show the mercy promised to our fathers and to
remember his holy covenant, the oath that he swore to our
father Abraham, to grant us that we, being delivered from the
hand of our enemies, might serve him without fear, in holiness
and righteousness before him all our days. And you, child, [that
is, John] will be called the prophet of the Most High; for you
will go before ***the Lord*** to prepare his ways to give knowledge
of salvation to his people in the forgiveness of their sins,
because of the tender mercy of our God, whereby the sunrise
shall visit us from on high to give light to those who sit in
darkness and in the shadow of death, to guide our feet into the
way of peace' (Luke 1:31-35,43,68-79).

And:

When they had crucified him, they divided his garments among
them by casting lots. Then they sat down and kept watch over
him there. And over his head they put the charge against him,
which read: 'This is Jesus, ***the King of the Jews***'. Then two
robbers were crucified with him, one on the right and one on
the left. And those who passed by derided him, wagging their
heads and saying: 'You who would destroy the temple and
rebuild it in three days, save yourself! If you are ***the Son of
God***, come down from the cross'. So also the chief priests, with
the scribes and elders, mocked him, saying: 'He saved others;
he cannot save himself. He is ***the King of Israel***; let him come
down now from the cross, and we will believe in him. He trusts
in God; let God deliver him now, if he desires him. For he said:
"I am the Son of God"'. And the robbers who were crucified
with him also reviled him in the same way (Matt. 27:35-44).

47

The kingdom was the major topic of Christ's ministry.[2] Use of a search engine will soon verify it. Consider these passages.

In preparing the way for Christ, John the Baptist (Isa. 40:3-5; Mal. 3:1-2; Luke 1:76-79; 7:27-28), as a herald, opened with the startling announcement of the imminence of the long-expected kingdom:

> John the Baptist came preaching in the wilderness of Judea: 'Repent, for the kingdom of heaven is at hand'. For this [that is John the Baptist] is he who was spoken of by the prophet Isaiah when he said: "The voice of one crying in the wilderness: 'Prepare the way of the Lord; make his paths straight'" (Matt. 3:1-3).

And Christ, following hard on John, confirmed his words:

> Jesus came into Galilee, proclaiming the gospel of God, and saying: 'The time is fulfilled, and the kingdom of God is at hand; repent and believe in the gospel' (Mark 1:14-15).

The kingdom! How did Christ begin the model prayer which showed his disciples how to pray? Like this:

> Father, hallowed be your name. Your kingdom come (Luke 11:2).

How did he respond to Nicodemus? Like this:

> Unless one is born again he cannot see the kingdom of God... he cannot enter the kingdom of God (John 3:3,6).

And so on. The Gospels are full of kingdom references.

One of the most significant – but most misunderstood – episodes in Christ's kingdom-ministry occurred even as he was undergoing the agony of Calvary; it was recorded by Luke

---

[2] See the series 'Thoughts on the Kingdom' on my sermonaudio.com page. George Eldon Ladd: 'The hope of the establishment of God's kingdom is the central theme of the prophets. It was also the central theme of Jesus' proclamation' (George Eldon Ladd: *I Believe in the Resurrection of Jesus*, William B.Eerdmans Publishing Company, Grand Rapids, 1975, p144). See also Gordon Fee: 'The Kingdom of God'.

(Luke 23:36-43). For centuries, men have debated the placing of the comma in Luke 23:43. This, however, badly misses the point. The fact is, there was no comma in the original – this kind of punctuation mark was only invented centuries after Luke wrote. Traditionally, this unassuming punctuation mark has been placed after 'you': 'I say to you, today you will be with me in paradise'. I have become convinced it should be thus: 'I say to you today, you will be with me in paradise'.[3]

The relevance of this seeming semantic – not to say, pedantic – digression lies in the fact that misplacing the comma leads to playing down the thought of the kingdom – which I have come to see as the main point of the passage – and playing up the thought of the intermediate state – which I have come to see as a theological (Christendom) import into the passage. This confusion bespeaks a serious loss.

Taking the argument about the comma for granted,[4] here is the relevant passage (properly punctuated):

> The soldiers also mocked [Christ], coming up and offering him sour wine and saying: 'If you are the King of the Jews, save yourself!' There was also an inscription over him: 'This is the King of the Jews'. One of the criminals who were hanged railed at him, saying: 'Are you not the Christ? Save yourself and us!' But the other rebuked him, saying, 'Do you not fear God, since you are under the same sentence of condemnation? And we indeed justly, for we are receiving the due reward of our deeds; but this man has done nothing wrong'. And he said: 'Jesus, remember me when you come into your kingdom'. And he said to him: 'Truly, I say to you today, you will be with me in paradise' (Luke 23:36-43).

The essence of the exchange between the thief and Christ was not heaven – heaven today, or whenever – but Christ as King, Christ's kingdom. Above all, the thief wanted to have a part in that kingdom. In other words, the thief had come to see Christ as a king, a king with a kingdom – *and he had come to see it on*

---

[3] For my full argument, see Appendix 2.
[4] See the previous note.

that particular day, at that dreadful time, under those wretched circumstances; and he openly said so! Remember that at the start of the agony he had joined his fellow thief in verbally abusing Christ (Mark 15:32). It follows therefore, that as he witnessed the way in which Christ was responding to the torment he was enduring, the thief's eyes – spiritually speaking – must have been opened. Moreover – as the proper punctuation of Christ's words brings out – 'Truly, I say to you today, you will be with me in paradise' – Christ gloriously endorsed the thief's discernment and faith *on that very day, under those most appalling and unpropitious circumstances*. If I may be permitted an accommodation of Luke 9:7, Christ's commendation of the centurion's faith might well be applied to the thief on the cross: 'I tell you, not even in Israel have I found such faith'. The leap is not too big. Compare the thief's evident faith with Pilate's apoplectic, sneering outburst when faced with Christ as king: 'You are a king, then!' (John 18:37). Surely, then, in the words of the thief, we have a very strong faith contrasted with a dismissive, political piece of sarcasm, scorn, derision and mockery.

How much did the thief understand when he addressed Christ as king? Did he fully appreciate what he was saying? I doubt it![5] Indeed, that is why I have used lower case for 'king' in the relevant text above. But then, believers so often have to confess

---

[5] Had James, John and their mother really weighed Christ's reference to his sufferings when they approached him with their request: 'Say that these two sons of mine are to sit, one at your right hand and one at your left, in your kingdom' (Matt. 20:17-21; Mark 10:32-37)? I doubt it. Calvin, I fear, in his *Commentary* on Matthew overstated the case: 'It was worthy of commendation in the sons of Zebedee that they expected some kingdom of Christ, of which not even the slightest trace was then visible. They see Christ exposed to contempt under the mean aspect of a servant; indeed more, they see him despised and loaded with many reproaches by the world; but they are convinced that he will soon become a magnificent king, for so he had taught them. It is unquestionably a noble specimen of faith'. To my mind, Calvin's words are more applicable to the thief – he spoke of the kingdom at the very time Christ was at his nadir, suffering such ignominy.

that they are guilty of saying things which go far beyond what their minds grasp and their hearts feel. Take hymn singing as a case in point: do we not all profess things which, in the cold light of day, go far beyond our experience, even, alas, beyond our real, heartfelt aspiration? What about our prayers? Which preacher stands guiltless? My guess is that the thief was in much the same boat here. (Indeed, some of us have to confess that we would be on a lower deck than he).

Nevertheless, I also think that we are justified in reminding ourselves just what the Jews felt about kingship. The thief had, however tenuously, been raised in that culture,[6] and, just as the average Briton today retains some vestiges of Christendom, so the thief might well have remembered snatches from the psalms dealing with kingship:

> O LORD, in your strength the king rejoices, and in your salvation how greatly he exults! You have given him his heart's desire and have not withheld the request of his lips... For you meet him with rich blessings; you set a crown of fine gold upon his head. He asked life of you; you gave it to him, length of days forever and ever. His glory is great through your salvation; splendour and majesty you bestow on him. For you make him most blessed forever; you make him glad with the joy of your presence. For the king trusts in the LORD, and through the steadfast love of the Most High he shall not be moved (Ps. 21:1-7).

> Kingship belongs to the LORD, and he rules over the nations (Ps. 22:28).

> Lift up your heads, O gates! And be lifted up, O ancient doors, that the King of glory may come in. Who is this King of glory? The LORD, strong and mighty, the LORD, mighty in battle! Lift up your heads, O gates! And lift them up, O ancient doors,

---

[6] I am taking it that the thief was a Jew. Of course, he might have been a Gentile. (As you may imagine, here is yet another fruitful topic for the speculators, and much ink has been spilled over its ins and outs). If he was not a Jew, his faith was even more remarkable – a Gentile, a pagan, who could, at that time, see Christ as king, one who had a kingdom?

that the King of glory may come in. Who is this King of glory? The LORD of hosts, he is the King of glory! (Ps. 24:7-10).

The LORD sits enthroned over the flood; the LORD sits enthroned as king forever (Ps. 29:10).

You are my King, O God; ordain salvation for Jacob! Through you we push down our foes; through your name we tread down those who rise up against us. For not in my bow do I trust, nor can my sword save me. But you have saved us from our foes and have put to shame those who hate us. In God we have boasted continually, and we will give thanks to your name forever (Ps. 44:4-8).

And so on. Supremely:

My heart overflows with a pleasing theme; I address my verses to the king; my tongue is like the pen of a ready scribe. You are the most handsome of the sons of men; grace is poured upon your lips; therefore God has blessed you forever. Gird your sword on your thigh, O mighty one, in your splendour and majesty! In your majesty ride out victoriously for the cause of truth and meekness and righteousness; let your right hand teach you awesome deeds! Your arrows are sharp in the heart of the king's enemies; the peoples fall under you. Your throne, O God, is forever and ever. The sceptre of your kingdom is a sceptre of uprightness; you have loved righteousness and hated wickedness. Therefore God, your God, has anointed you with the oil of gladness beyond your companions; your robes are all fragrant with myrrh and aloes and cassia. From ivory palaces stringed instruments make you glad; daughters of kings are among your ladies of honour; at your right hand stands the queen in gold of Ophir. Hear, O daughter, and consider, and incline your ear: forget your people and your father's house, and the king will desire your beauty. Since he is your lord, bow to him. The people of Tyre will seek your favour with gifts, the richest of the people. All glorious is the princess in her chamber, with robes interwoven with gold. In many-collared robes she is led to the king, with her virgin companions following behind her. With joy and gladness they are led along as they enter the palace of the king. In place of your fathers shall be your sons; you will make them princes in all the earth. I will cause your name to be remembered in all generations; therefore nations will praise you forever and ever (Ps. 45:1-17).

And:

> I will extol you, my God and King, and bless your name
> forever and ever. Every day I will bless you and praise your
> name forever and ever. Great is the LORD, and greatly to be
> praised, and his greatness is unsearchable. One generation shall
> commend your works to another, and shall declare your mighty
> acts. On the glorious splendour of your majesty, and on your
> wondrous works, I will meditate. They shall speak of the might
> of your awesome deeds, and I will declare your greatness. They
> shall pour forth the fame of your abundant goodness and shall
> sing aloud of your righteousness.
> The LORD is gracious and merciful, slow to anger and
> abounding in steadfast love. The LORD is good to all, and his
> mercy is over all that he has made. All your works shall give
> thanks to you, O LORD, and all your saints shall bless you!
> They shall speak of the glory of your kingdom and tell of your
> power, to make known to the children of man your mighty
> deeds, and the glorious splendour of your kingdom. Your
> kingdom is an everlasting kingdom, and your dominion
> endures throughout all generations. [The LORD is faithful in
> all his words and kind in all his works]. The LORD upholds all
> who are falling and raises up all who are bowed down. The
> eyes of all look to you, and you give them their food in due
> season. You open your hand; you satisfy the desire of every
> living thing. The LORD is righteous in all his ways and kind in
> all his works. The LORD is near to all who call on him, to all
> who call on him in truth. He fulfils the desire of those who fear
> him; he also hears their cry and saves them. The LORD
> preserves all who love him, but all the wicked he will destroy.
> My mouth will speak the praise of the LORD, and let all flesh
> bless his holy name forever and ever (Ps. 145:1-21).

It is not without significance that, speaking about the Lord
Jesus, the writer of the letter to the Hebrews actually quoted
some of those very words:

> 'Your throne, O God, is forever and ever, the sceptre of
> uprightness is the sceptre of your kingdom. You have loved
> righteousness and hated wickedness; therefore God, your God,
> has anointed you with the oil of gladness beyond your
> companions'. And: 'You, Lord, laid the foundation of the earth
> in the beginning, and the heavens are the work of your hands;
> they will perish, but you remain; they will all wear out like a

garment, like a robe you will roll them up, like a garment they will be changed. But you are the same, and your years will have no end'.
And to which of the angels has he ever said: 'Sit at my right hand until I make your enemies a footstool for your feet'? (Heb. 1:8-13).

Whether or not the thief had reached the depth of understanding which gripped the writer to the Hebrews in this, I cannot say; I doubt it. But then, does any believer? Let me make a dangerous suggestion: did the writer to the Hebrews fully appreciate it in all its ramifications?

Even so, this is what Luke 23:43 is all about. Whether or not the thief knew Daniel's prophecy:

The God of heaven will set up a kingdom that shall never be destroyed, nor shall the kingdom be left to another people. It shall break in pieces all these kingdoms and bring them to an end, and it shall stand forever (Dan. 2:44)...

To him [that is, Christ] was given dominion and glory and a kingdom, that all peoples, nations, and languages should serve him; his dominion is an everlasting dominion, which shall not pass away, and his kingdom one that shall not be destroyed (Dan. 7:14)...

...if he had lived, the thief would not have been surprised to read John's words from Patmos:

There were loud voices in heaven, saying: 'The kingdom of the world has become the kingdom of our Lord and of his Christ, and he shall reign forever and ever'.
And the twenty-four elders who sit on their thrones before God fell on their faces and worshipped God, saying: 'We give thanks to you, Lord God Almighty, who is and who was, for you have taken your great power and begun to reign. The nations raged, but your wrath came, and the time for the dead to be judged and for rewarding your servants, the prophets and saints, and those who fear your name both small and great, and for destroying the destroyers of the earth'.
Then God's temple in heaven was opened, and the ark of his covenant was seen within his temple. There were flashes of

lightning, rumblings, peals of thunder, an earthquake, and heavy hail (Rev. 11:15-19).

Now the salvation and the power and the kingdom of our God and the authority of his Christ have come (Rev. 12:10).

Those who had conquered the beast and its image and the number of its name... sing the song of Moses, the servant of God, and the song of the Lamb, saying: 'Great and amazing are your deeds, O Lord God the Almighty! Just and true are your ways, O King of the nations! Who will not fear, O Lord, and glorify your name? For you alone are holy. All nations will come and worship you, for your righteous acts have been revealed' (Rev. 15:2-4).

[The enemies of God and his people] will make war on the Lamb, and the Lamb will conquer them, for he is Lord of lords and King of kings, and those with him are called and chosen and faithful (Rev. 17:14).

Then I saw heaven opened, and behold, a white horse! The one sitting on it is called Faithful and True, and in righteousness he judges and makes war. His eyes are like a flame of fire, and on his head are many diadems, and he has a name written that no one knows but himself. He is clothed in a robe dipped in blood, and the name by which he is called is The Word of God. And the armies of heaven, arrayed in fine linen, white and pure, were following him on white horses. From his mouth comes a sharp sword with which to strike down the nations, and he will rule them with a rod of iron. He will tread the winepress of the fury of the wrath of God the Almighty. On his robe and on his thigh he has a name written, King of kings and Lord of lords (Rev. 19:11-16).[7]

Before I leave the Calvary exchange between the thief and Christ, let me make a (very) tentative suggestion. Consider Christ's statement, made not long before Calvary:

Truly, I say to you, there are some standing here who will not taste death until they see the Son of Man coming in his kingdom (Matt. 16:28).

---

[7] And victory – the victory and triumph of Christ over all his and his people's enemies – is the outcome (Rev. 19:6-21).

Is it possible that the thief was one of those Christ was speaking of? Christ's statement is almost always taken in the most literal sense. Is it possible we should view it as comparable to his statement to the Jews regarding the faith of Abraham? Christ declared:

> Your father Abraham rejoiced that he would see my day. He saw it and was glad (John 8:56).

In other words, by faith Abraham (I am convinced it was in the substitution of the ram for Isaac in sacrifice recorded in Genesis 22:1-19) saw Christ and his work – dimly, no doubt – but he saw the day of Christ; that is, in his case, Christ's accomplishment of redemption. Moreover, he longed for it – that is the meaning of Christ's words.[8] The same could be said about the thief with his desire to be a part of Christ's kingdom.

It might well be argued that kingship was the core issue at the crucifixion,[9] certainly as far as Luke was concerned. (And not only when writing his Gospel; see below, for Acts). This, of course, dovetails with the fact (already noted) that the kingdom was the major topic of Christ's ministry.

Luke was not alone in emphasising the kingdom as *the* issue at the crucifixion. The Jewish bigwigs saw it. Pilate saw it. The soldiers and the crowd saw it. The thief saw it, and that was the truly remarkable thing![10] Consider Luke's record:

> Then the whole company of them arose and brought him [that is, Christ] before Pilate. And they began to accuse him, saying: 'We found this man misleading our nation and forbidding us to give tribute to Caesar, and saying that he himself is Christ, a *king*'. And Pilate asked him: 'Are you the *King* of the Jews?'... The soldiers also mocked him, coming up and offering him sour wine and saying: 'If you are the *King* of the Jews, save

---

[8] See my discourse on John 8:56, 'Longing Anticipation', on my sermonaudio.com page.

[9] Christ made it clear to the disciples at the final Passover (Matt. 26:29; Mark 14:25; Luke 22:16-18,29-30).

[10] All this makes it even more remarkable (sadly remarkable) that contemporary evangelicals often miss it altogether.

yourself!' There was also an inscription over him, 'This is the *King* of the Jews'.

One of the criminals who were hanged railed at him, saying: 'Are you not the Christ? Save yourself and us!' But the other rebuked him, saying: 'Do you not fear God, since you are under the same sentence of condemnation? And we indeed justly, for we are receiving the due reward of our deeds; but this man has done nothing wrong'. And he said: 'Jesus, remember me when you come into your *kingdom'*. And he said to him: 'Truly, I say to you today, you will be with me in paradise' (Luke 23:1-3,36-43).

And we have John's account:

Pilate entered his headquarters again and called Jesus and said to him: 'Are you the *King* of the Jews?' Jesus answered: 'Do you say this of your own accord, or did others say it to you about me?' Pilate answered: 'Am I a Jew? Your own nation and the chief priests have delivered you over to me. What have you done?' Jesus answered: 'My *kingdom* is not of this world. If my *kingdom* were of this world, my servants would have been fighting, that I might not be delivered over to the Jews. But my *kingdom* is not from the world'. Then Pilate said to him: 'So you are a *king*?' Jesus answered: 'You say that I am a *king*. For this purpose I was born and for this purpose I have come into the world – to bear witness to the truth. Everyone who is of the truth listens to my voice'. Pilate said to him: 'What is truth?' (John 18:33-38).

Then Pilate took Jesus and flogged him. And the soldiers twisted together a crown of thorns and put it on his head and arrayed him in a purple robe. They came up to him, saying: 'Hail, *King* of the Jews!' and struck him with their hands (John 19:1-3).

Pilate sought to release him, but the Jews cried out: 'If you release this man, you are not Caesar's friend. Everyone who makes himself a *king* opposes Caesar'. So when Pilate heard these words, he brought Jesus out and sat down on the judgment seat at a place called The Stone Pavement, and in Aramaic Gabbatha. Now it was the day of Preparation of the Passover. It was about the sixth hour. He said to the Jews: 'Behold your *King*!' They cried out: 'Away with him, away with him, crucify him!' Pilate said to them: 'Shall I crucify your *King*?' The chief priests answered: 'We have no *king* but

Caesar'. So he delivered him over to them to be crucified (John 19:12-16).

Pilate also wrote an inscription and put it on the cross. It read: 'Jesus of Nazareth, the **King** of the Jews'. Many of the Jews read this inscription, for the place where Jesus was crucified was near the city, and it was written in Aramaic, in Latin, and in Greek. So the chief priests of the Jews said to Pilate: 'Do not write: "The **King** of the Jews", but rather: "This man said, I am **King** of the Jews". Pilate answered: 'What I have written I have written' (John 19:19-22).

And Mark:

Pilate asked [Jesus]: 'Are you the **King** of the Jews?' And he answered him: 'You have said so'... [Pilate asked the crowd]: 'Do you want me to release for you the **King** of the Jews?'... Pilate again said to them: 'Then what shall I do with the man you call the **King** of the Jews?'... [The soldiers] began to salute [Jesus]: 'Hail, **King** of the Jews!'... The inscription of the charge against him read: 'The **King** of the Jews'... The chief priests with the scribes mocked him to one another, saying: 'He saved others; he cannot save himself. Let the Christ, the **King** of Israel, come down now from the cross that we may see and believe'... Joseph of Arimathea, a respected member of the council, who was also himself looking for the **kingdom** of God, took courage and went to Pilate and asked for the body of Jesus (Mark 15:2,9,12,18,26,31-32,43).

Nor should we forget Matthew's contribution; his Gospel might well be described as 'The Gospel of the Kingdom'.[11]

Luke made sure we did not miss it. Having published his Gospel – with its emphasis on the kingdom – look how he opened Acts, his follow-up volume. As he explained, after Christ's resurrection the kingdom was never far below the surface for the *ekklēsia*. Far beneath the surface? As we have seen, it was the very topic which Christ chose when teaching his disciples in the days following his resurrection:

---

[11] The title C.H.Spurgeon gave to his commentary on Matthew. See also my *Smoke*.

He presented himself alive to them after his suffering by many
proofs, appearing to them during forty days and speaking about
the *kingdom* of God (Acts 1:3).

And the disciples, although they were utterly at sea about it,
were nevertheless deeply interested in the subject.
Understandably so! Had they not been raised in a culture of
Messianic-kingdom expectation, this hope having been
repeatedly stimulated by the reading of the prophets? This was
the background to their question:

> So when they had come together, they asked him: 'Lord, will
> you at this time restore the *kingdom* to Israel?' (Acts 1:6).

Christ immediately set them on the right course:

> It is not for you to know times or seasons that the Father has
> fixed by his own authority. But you will receive power when
> the Holy Spirit has come upon you, and you will be my
> witnesses in Jerusalem and in all Judea and Samaria, and to the
> end of the earth (Acts 1:7-8).

Moreover, having witnessed Christ's ascension into glory, they
were tempted to stand staring (no doubt) open-mouthed into the
sky. Heavenly messengers quickly disabused them, however:

> Men of Galilee, why do you stand looking into heaven? This
> Jesus, who was taken up from you into heaven, will come in
> the same way as you saw him go into heaven (Acts 1:11).

In other words: 'Christ will return; meanwhile, you need to get
on with kingdom work, including the preaching of the
resurrected Christ!' You have been taught to pray for the
coming of the kingdom (Matt. 6:10), and commanded to preach
the gospel to advance the kingdom (Matt. 28:18-20), so... when
you are empowered, get on with it!

They got the message. In a very short while they were thinking
of a replacement for Judas, looking for one who would be 'a
witness to [Christ's] resurrection' taking the traitor's 'place in
this ministry and apostleship' (Acts 1:21-26).

And on the day of Pentecost, following hard on Christ's
bestowal of the Spirit, the new covenant now being fully

established, Peter (I am sure to his amazement) found himself majestically proclaiming the glorious truth of the resurrection. No! Let me express it more accurately. Peter did not lecture on a doctrine, consulting previously prepared notes: as a town crier, he simply stood and proclaimed a person – the person of Jesus, the crucified, resurrected and ascended Messiah and King. David, he thundered, being:

> ...a prophet, and knowing that God had sworn with an oath to him that he would set one of his descendants on his throne... foresaw and spoke about the resurrection of the Christ... that he was not abandoned to Hades, nor did his flesh see corruption. This Jesus God raised up, and of that we all are witnesses. Being therefore exalted at the right hand of God, and having received from the Father the promise of the Holy Spirit, he has poured out this that you yourselves are seeing and hearing (Acts 2:30-33).

And that was only the start of it! From that point on, the kingdom with Christ as the risen King was the constant theme of the apostolic ministry. How frequent are the references to the kingdom in the post-Pentecost Scriptures! Take Luke's follow-up volume (Acts 1:3,6; 8:12; 14:22; 17:7; 19:8; 20:25; 28:23,31). Take the rest of the apostolic Scriptures (Rom. 14:17; 1 Cor. 4:8,20; 1 Cor. 6:9-10; 15:24,50; Gal. 5:21; Eph. 5:5; Col. 1:13; 4:11; 1 Thess. 2:12; 2 Thess. 1:5; 1 Tim. 1:17; 6:14-16; 2 Tim. 4:1,18; Heb. 1:8; 7:1-2; 12:28; Jas. 2:5; 2 Pet. 1:11; Revelation *passim*). And it's to be seen not only in direct 'kingdom' references but in all the scriptural allusions to Christ's reign, kingship and rule, and, of course, the believer's reign in Christ (Matt. 25:20-21; Luke 22:28-30; Rom. 5:17,21; 1 Cor. 6:3; Eph. 2:6; 2 Tim. 2:12; Rev. 1:6 with 5:10; 20:1-6).

Until I was writing this book I had not sufficiently appreciated the role played by Melchizedek in the link between Christ's kingship and his priesthood, especially regarding what I am trying to say here. Consider the way the writer to the Hebrews argued:

> We who have fled [to Christ] for refuge... have strong encouragement to hold fast to the hope set before us. We have

this as a sure and steadfast anchor of the soul, a hope that enters into the inner place behind the curtain, where Jesus has gone as a forerunner on our behalf, having become a high priest forever after the order of Melchizedek (Heb. 6:18-20).

That is to say, believers have a hope – a certain, confident expectation – which is entirely bound up in the person of Christ, especially his permanent, heavenly priesthood following his life, death, resurrection and ascension into glory. The writer to the Hebrews, having introduced Melchizedek as typical of Christ in this respect, immediately develops the point he wants to make:

For this Melchizedek, king of Salem, priest of the Most High God, met Abraham returning from the slaughter of the kings and blessed him, and to him Abraham apportioned a tenth part of everything. He is first, by translation of his name, king of righteousness, and then he is also king of Salem, that is, king of peace. He is without father or mother or genealogy, having neither beginning of days nor end of life, but resembling the Son of God he continues a priest forever (Heb. 7:1-3).

The material point is, of course, that in the old covenant no man could be both king and priest (Ex. 3:10; 16:40; 2 Chron. 26:18; witness the sin of Jeroboam in 1 Kings 12:25 – 13:6). In the new covenant, however, not only is Christ both King *and* great High Priest, all his people in him are both kings and priests (1 Pet. 2:4-10; Rev. 1:6; 5:10; 20:6). No wonder then, that the writer to the Hebrews made so much of the change of covenant brought about by Christ:

Now if perfection had been attainable through the levitical priesthood (for under it the people received the law), what further need would there have been for another priest to arise after the order of Melchizedek, rather than one named after the order of Aaron? For when there is a change in the priesthood, there is necessarily a change in the law as well. For the one of whom these things are spoken belonged to another tribe, from which no one has ever served at the altar. For it is evident that our Lord was descended from Judah, and in connection with that tribe Moses said nothing about priests. This becomes even more evident when another priest arises in the likeness of Melchizedek, who has become a priest, not on the basis of a legal requirement concerning bodily descent, but by the power of an indestructible life. For it is witnessed of him: 'You are a priest forever, after the order of Melchizedek' (Heb. 7:11-17).

And so to the contrast between the covenants:

> The former [that is, levitical] priests were many in number, because they were prevented by death from continuing in office, but he [that is, Christ] holds his priesthood permanently, because he continues forever. Consequently, he is able to save to the uttermost those who draw near to God through him, since he always lives to make intercession for them. For it was indeed fitting that we should have such a high priest, holy, innocent, unstained, separated from sinners, and exalted above the heavens (Heb. 7:23-26).

The writer sums it up:

> Now the point in what we are saying is this: we have such a high priest, one who is seated at the right hand of the throne of the Majesty in heaven (Heb. 8:1).

No wonder then that the writer could say:

> In speaking of a new covenant, he [that is, God speaking through Jeremiah the prophet] makes the first one obsolete (Heb. 8:13).

* * *

When will the kingdom actually come? I do not ask this question out of carnal curiosity, or to kick start an orgy of speculation. Far from it. It has a huge bearing on what I am trying to say in this book. When will the kingdom come?

John the Baptist immediately pre-dated the coming of the kingdom:

> What then did you go out to see? A prophet? Yes, I tell you, and more than a prophet. This is he of whom it is written: 'Behold, I send my messenger before your face, who will prepare your way before you'. I tell you, among those born of women none is greater than John. Yet the one who is least in the kingdom of God is greater than he (Luke 7:26-28).

The law and the prophets were until John; since then the good news of the kingdom of God is preached, and everyone forces his way into it (Luke 16:16).

As we have seen, in preparing the people of Israel for Christ, John the Baptist was explicit about the imminence of the kingdom (Matt. 3:1-3), and Christ himself, in opening his ministry, immediately confirmed John's assurance (Mark 1:14-15). Moreover, some time later, when the Pharisees wanted to know when the kingdom would come, Christ declared:

> The kingdom of God is in the midst of you [that is, among you, or within your grasp] (Luke 17:21).

As he had announced earlier:

> The kingdom of God has come upon you (Luke 11:20).

So far, so good; the kingdom was already here, with Christ when he was on earth. But when would the kingdom come in its fullness? And what would that fullness be? What would mark it? Christ's incarnation had been obscure, lowly, almost secret (except to some favoured few) – would it be the same when he brought in the kingdom in all its glory? John the Baptist, in preparing Israel for the first coming of Christ, had included an intriguing prophecy; speaking in apocalyptic terms, he declared:

> His winnowing fork is in his hand, and he will clear his threshing floor and gather his wheat into the barn, but the chaff he will burn with unquenchable fire (Matt. 3:12).

And this, of course, was just as the prophet had foretold:

> Behold, I send my messenger, and he will prepare the way before me. And the Lord whom you seek will suddenly come to his temple; and the messenger of the covenant in whom you delight, behold, he is coming, says the LORD of hosts. But who can endure the day of his coming, and who can stand when he appears? For he is like a refiner's fire and like fullers' soap (Mal. 3:1-2).

But this winnowing ministry, in the fullest sense, did not form part of Christ's ministry when he was on earth.[12] So what did Christ say about this aspect of his kingdom, his ministry of judgment and final, eternal separation of all men? He made it clear that while his first coming was to redeem his people from their sin:

> God did not send his Son into the world to condemn the world, but in order that the world might be saved through him (John 3:17; see also John 8:15; 12:47)...

...his second coming would be very different. In the Parable of the Talents, he explained to those who 'supposed that the kingdom of God was to appear immediately' that it was not so: he would be going away in order 'to receive for himself a kingdom and then return' – and return as judge:

> When he returned, having received the kingdom, he ordered these servants to whom he had given the money to be called to him, that he might know what they had gained by doing business.

After various awards to his people, the king will turn to his enemies:

> As for these enemies of mine, who did not want me to reign over them, bring them here and slaughter them before me (Luke 19:11-27).

Again:

> When the Son of Man comes in his glory, and all the angels with him, then he will sit on his glorious throne. Before him will be gathered all the nations, and he will separate people one from another as a shepherd separates the sheep from the goats.

---

[12] This surprised John – or was he asking for his disciples? So much so: 'When John heard in prison about the deeds of the Christ, he sent word by his disciples and said to him: "Are you the one who is to come, or shall we look for another?" And Jesus answered them: "Go and tell John what you hear and see: the blind receive their sight and the lame walk, lepers are cleansed and the deaf hear, and the dead are raised up, and the poor have good news preached to them. And blessed is the one who is not offended by me"' (Matt. 11:2-6).

And he will place the sheep on his right, but the goats on the left. Then the King will say to those on his right: 'Come, you who are blessed by my Father, inherit the kingdom prepared for you from the foundation of the world...' (Matt. 25:31-34).

And, speaking of two 'hearings' – the hearing in regeneration and the hearing at the trumpet call for the final resurrection – Christ asserted:

Truly, truly, I say to you, an hour is coming, and is now here, when the dead will hear the voice of the Son of God, and those who hear will live. For as the Father has life in himself, so he has granted the Son also to have life in himself. And he has given him authority to execute judgment, because he is the Son of Man. Do not marvel at this, for an hour is coming when all who are in the tombs will hear his voice and come out, those who have done good to the resurrection of life, and those who have done evil to the resurrection of judgment (John 5:25-29).

As Paul, writing to believers, would later put it:

Since we believe that Jesus died and rose again, even so, through Jesus, God will bring with him those who have fallen asleep. For this we declare to you by a word from the Lord, that we who are alive, who are left until the coming of the Lord, will not precede those who have fallen asleep. For the Lord himself will descend from heaven with a cry of command, with the voice of an archangel, and with the sound of the trumpet of God. And the dead in Christ will rise first. Then we who are alive, who are left, will be caught up together with them in the clouds to meet the Lord in the air, and so we will always be with the Lord. Therefore encourage one another with these words. Now concerning the times and the seasons, brothers, you have no need to have anything written to you. For you yourselves are fully aware that the day of the Lord will come like a thief in the night. While people are saying: 'There is peace and security', then sudden destruction will come upon them as labour pains come upon a pregnant woman, and they will not escape (1 Thess. 4:14 – 5:3).

Your steadfastness and faith in all your persecutions and in the afflictions that you are enduring... is evidence of the righteous judgment of God, that you may be considered worthy of the kingdom of God, for which you are also suffering – since indeed God considers it just to repay with affliction those who afflict you, and to grant relief to you who are afflicted as well as to us, when the Lord Jesus is revealed from heaven with his mighty angels in flaming fire, inflicting vengeance on those who do not know God and on those who do not obey the gospel of our Lord Jesus... Now concerning the coming of our Lord Jesus Christ and our being gathered together to him... (2 Thess. 1:4-8; 2:1).

But, of course, all that was long in the future. Meanwhile:

When Christ had offered for all time a single sacrifice for sins, he sat down at the right hand of God, waiting from that time until his enemies should be made a footstool for his feet (Heb. 10:12-13).

But that time – the bringing in of the kingdom in all its fullness – will come:

Then I saw a new heaven and a new earth, for the first heaven and the first earth had passed away, and the sea was no more. And I saw the holy city, new Jerusalem, coming down out of heaven from God, prepared as a bride adorned for her husband. And I heard a loud voice from the throne saying: 'Behold, the dwelling place of God is with man. He will dwell with them, and they will be his people, and God himself will be with them as their God. He will wipe away every tear from their eyes, and death shall be no more, neither shall there be mourning, nor crying, nor pain anymore, for the former things have passed away'. And he who was seated on the throne said: 'Behold, I am making all things new' (Rev. 21:1-4).

As Christ declared:

Behold, I am coming soon, bringing my recompense with me, to repay each one for what he has done (Rev. 22:12).

In short, the kingdom will come in all its fullness at the return of Christ, with the resurrection of all men (either to eternal life or eternal damnation), and only then. The important point here is that Christ's resurrection and kingdom are intimately connected in Scripture. Moreover – and this has a vital bearing on what I am trying to say – the two were major and constant themes of the first believers. And, as we have seen, the resurrection of

Christ was key to it all. I have already quoted Peter's preaching on the day of Pentecost. I return to that discourse:

...the resurrection of the Christ... This Jesus God raised up, and of that we all are witnesses. Being therefore exalted at the right hand of God, and having received from the Father the promise of the Holy Spirit, he has poured out this that you yourselves are seeing and hearing... Let all the house of Israel therefore know for certain that God has made him both Lord and Christ, this Jesus whom you crucified (Acts 2:29-36).

And so, as they had begun, so the apostles continued:

And with great power the apostles were giving their testimony to the resurrection of the Lord Jesus (Acts 4:33).

And so on.

As for the apostolic letters, just one example for now; namely Paul's opening of his letter to the Romans:

...[Paul] a servant of Christ Jesus, called to be an apostle, set apart for the gospel of God, which he promised beforehand through his prophets in the holy Scriptures, concerning his Son, who was descended from David according to the flesh and was declared to be the Son of God in power according to the Spirit of holiness by his resurrection from the dead, Jesus Christ our Lord, through whom we have received grace and apostleship to bring about the obedience of faith for the sake of his name among all the nations, including you who are called to belong to Jesus Christ (Rom. 1:1-6).[13]

Clearly, it is not merely that – as a historical fact – that Christ rose from the dead, but that by his resurrection he openly declared himself to be the Son of God, the true and only King. Tyrants, emperors, dictators, and the like can torment and kill

---

[13] Remember the high priest's demand at Christ's trial: 'I adjure you by the living God, tell us if you are the Christ, the Son of God' and Jesus' answer: 'You will see the Son of Man seated at the right hand of power and coming on the clouds of heaven' (Matt. 26:63-64). Here in Rom. 1:1-6 we have a major contribution to that riposte: 'Jesus Christ our Lord' 'was declared to be the Son of God in power according to the Spirit of holiness by his resurrection from the dead'.

the body, but God alone controls the destiny of the entire man, of every man (not excluding tyrants!) (Matt. 10:28); Christ has conquered death – the tyrant's ultimate sanction. And the first believers made sure the world faced this fact, and faced it fair and square; the hostile cultures surrounding the early *ekklēsia* were never allowed to forget it. It was no cosy dollop of syrup that believers held out to unbelievers: they had crucified the Christ; but Christ was raised; Christ was King; Christ was coming back; all men had to face him; get ready! The hostile cultures got the message, and they didn't like it! Hence conflict was inevitable when the saints preached the resurrected Christ *in* a hostile world, and preached the resurrected Christ *to* a hostile world – which they knew they had to do.

Paul made this very clear: Christ 'was declared to be the Son of God in power according to the Spirit of holiness by his resurrection from the dead, Jesus Christ our Lord' (Rom. 1:4), he declared. Clearly, the resurrection – and its inevitable consequence, Christ as the Son of God, the Lord, the King – was not some choice morsel of esoteric knowledge to be hidden within the confines of the *ekklēsia* – some special, secret insight reserved for the elite, the elect: it – indeed, – Christ himself – was to be proclaimed, and proclaimed as publicly as possible, not apologetically, but in triumph: 'What we proclaim is... Jesus Christ as Lord' (2 Cor. 4:5). With the death and resurrection of Christ, a new day had dawned, opening a new age, with a new covenant, a new kingdom in which every believer will, at the last Day, receive a new, immortal body like Christ's, to live forever in bliss in a new heaven and a new earth, where the Lord Jesus Christ will be eternally exalted for his complete victory over sin, and death, and the utter eradication of all evil in every shape and form and consequence. David Pawson made a telling rhetorical point:

> The word 'new' hardly ever occurs in the Old Testament. The
> only text that springs readily to mind is: 'There is nothing new

under the sun' (Eccles. 1:9). Yet the New Testament is full of the word. What has caused the change?[14]

The new covenant, of course, inaugurated by Christ's resurrection and bestowal of the Spirit!

As just noted, Paul opened his letter to the Romans by describing himself and his ministry in terms of the resurrection of Christ in accordance with the promise of the prophets (Rom. 1:1-6). And he virtually closed the letter with (quoting, respectively, 2 Samuel 22:50; Psalm 18:49; Deuteronomy 32:43; Psalm 117:1; Isaiah 11:10):

> I tell you that Christ became a servant to the circumcised to show God's truthfulness, in order to confirm the promises given to the patriarchs, and in order that the Gentiles might glorify God for his mercy. As it is written: 'Therefore I will praise you among the Gentiles, and sing to your name'.
> And again it is said: 'Rejoice, O Gentiles, with his people'.
> And again: 'Praise the Lord, all you Gentiles, and let all the peoples extol him'.
> And again Isaiah says: 'The root of Jesse will come, even he who arises to rule the Gentiles; in him will the Gentiles hope'.
> May the God of hope fill you with all joy and peace in believing, so that by the power of the Holy Spirit you may abound in hope (Rom. 15:8-13).

Christ's resurrection proved that he was indeed the Messiah, and that all the promises were or would be fulfilled in him. The fact is, if Christ has not been raised, there can be no kingdom, there is no resurrection for the believer; it is all a delusion, a pipedream.[15]

---

[14] J.David Pawson: *Explaining The Resurrection*, Sovereign World, Tonbridge, 1993, p50.

[15] Norman L.Geisler on why it essential to maintain that Christ rose with the same physical body as he had from his incarnation: 'Anything less than the resurrection of the material body [of Christ] would not restore God's perfect material creation, including mankind. Hence, an immaterial resurrection is contrary to God's creative purposes. Just as God will recreate the material universe (Rev. 21:1-4; 2 Pet. 3:10-13) in redeeming the old one, even so he will reconstitute the material body in redeeming the one that died. Anything short of a material recreation of

Daniel P.Fuller:

> The New Testament conceives of the resurrection of Jesus as the basis for all of the events of redemptive history... 'Thus the resurrection becomes the fulcrum of theology'... 'When once we grasp clearly the momentous interests which are involved in the belief in the resurrection, we shall be prepared to understand how it formed the central point of the apostolic teachings; and yet more than this, how the event itself is the central point of history'.[16]

No wonder! The Father and the Son and the Spirit are all and each involved in the resurrection[17] – thus giving the resurrection a vital role in the early believers' understanding of the triune God, with, especially, Christ as the Son of God. His name to them was 'Immanuel... God with us' (Matt. 1:23); he was 'God... manifested in the flesh' (1 Tim. 3:16). This, of course, dominated their preaching of the gospel.

---

the world and a material reconstruction of the body would spell failure for God's creative purpose... Without a physical resurrection there is no ground for celebrating Christ's victory over physical death... Unless Christ rose in the flesh, his full human nature was not restored, and he is not our divine/human Mediator (1 Tim. 2:5)... It is only through [his] physical resurrection that Christ has "destroyed death and has brought life and immortality to light through the gospel" (2 Tim. 1:10). Paul told the Corinthians: "If Christ has not been raised... those who have fallen asleep in Christ are lost" (1 Cor. 15:17-18)... If Jesus' resurrection body was only an immaterial body, then [he] was knowingly misleading his disciples [when he met them again after his resurrection – see Luke 24; John 20]. That is, he was intentionally leading them to believe what he knew was not true. In short, if Jesus' resurrection body was not a physical, material body, then he was lying... Unless Jesus rose in a material body, there is no way to verify his resurrection. It loses its historically persuasive value' ('It Makes a Difference', in Norman L.Geisler: *The Battle for the Resurrection*, Thomas Nelson, Nashville, 1989, pp30-39, especially pp33-36).

[16] Daniel P.Fuller: *Easter Faith and History*, The Tyndale Press, London, 1968, p19, quoting Walter Künneth and B.F.Westcott.

[17] For more on this, see Peter Masters: 'Eight Purposes and Lessons in the Resurrection', *Sword & Trowel*, number 4, 1993, pp12-13.

No resurrection? No hope! The kingdom prophecies made null and void. Paul made this clear when facing the Jewish council:

> Now when Paul perceived that one part were Sadducees and the other Pharisees, he cried out in the council: 'Brothers, I am a Pharisee, a son of Pharisees. It is with respect to the hope and the resurrection of the dead that I am on trial' (Acts 23:6).

* * *

Having dealt with this in general terms, let us now sharpen the focus. In specific terms, how did the early believers make use of 'resurrection' and 'kingdom'? What did these things mean to them – in detail?

What follows can be thought of under three main headings: Confrontation, Consecration and Comfort.

I start with the first believers' attitude to unbelievers. How did the early *ekklēsia* use the Kingship of Christ in their approach to those who were trapped in cultures hostile to Christ and his gospel? One word epitomises it: Confrontation.[18] Proving it takes us to the next chapter.

---

[18] See my *To Confront; Evangelical Dilemma*.

Use 1: Confrontation

Throughout its history, Israel, having been drawn out of Egypt, was always to be a separated people in the midst of idolatry. Moreover, God had always confronted that idolatry through his people:

> You are my witnesses... and my servant whom I have chosen, that you may know and believe me and understand that I am he. Before me no god was formed, nor shall there be any after me. I, I am the LORD, and besides me there is no Saviour. I declared and saved and proclaimed, when there was no strange god among you; and you are my witnesses... and I am God. Also henceforth I am he; there is none who can deliver from my hand; I work, and who can turn it back?... Fear not, nor be afraid; have I not told you from of old and declared it? And you are my witnesses! Is there a God besides me? There is no Rock; I know not any (Isa. 43:10-13; 44:8).

Indeed, God made Israel confront idolatry, especially whenever it tried to cross Israel's borders; above all, when any in Israel itself went looking for idolatry. Prophet after prophet proclaimed against it. The Mosaic covenant demanded Israel's absolute separation from it, complete separation from paganism; fully-committed devotion to the one true God, the God of Israel, was the order of the day for Israel.[1]

So much for Israel and the old covenant. The material point for the new covenant, however, is that believers have to learn from Israel's history (1 Cor. 10:1-14): 'These things happened to them as an example, but they were written down for our instruction, on whom the end of the ages has come' (1 Cor. 10:11). And not only instruction: 'Therefore, my beloved, flee from idolatry' (1 Cor. 10:14). Flee idolatry! Just as Israel had to

---

[1] See, for instance, Ex. 20:1-8; 23:13; Lev. 19:4; Deut. 7:25; 12:32 – 13:18; 27:15; Judg. 10:14; 1 Sam. 15:23; Ps. 16:4; 115:1-18; 135:15-18; Isa. 2:8; 42:17; 44:9-20; 45:20; Jer. 1:16; 7:18; 10:3-16; Dan. 5:23; Hos. 11:2; Mic. 5:13; Jonah 2:8; Hab. 2:18, and so on.

flee from idolatry, separate from it and its devotees, so for the *ekklēsia*; separation from the world and its idolatry is a hallmark of the *ekklēsia* in the new covenant.[2] Idolatry is always an abomination which arouses the wrath of God – both it and its perpetrators (Rom. 1:23; 1 Cor. 6:9; 10:7,14,19; Gal. 4:8; 5:19-20; Eph. 5:5; Col. 3:5; 1 John 5:21; Rev. 19:20; 21:18).[3]

Pagans, even educated pagans, are idolaters:

> While Paul was waiting... at Athens, his spirit was provoked within him as he saw that the city was full of idols (Acts 17:16).

The same goes for the *hoi polloi*. As the apostle reminded the Corinthians:

> You know that when you were pagans you were led astray to mute idols (1 Cor. 12:2).

Ah, ancient Greece! Of course! What can you expect?

Oh no! There is more to idolatry – far more – than carving a chunk of wood, chiselling some marble, or erecting a temple. When writing to the Galatians, Paul spelled out what he meant by it:

> The works of the flesh are evident: sexual immorality, impurity, sensuality, idolatry, sorcery, enmity, strife, jealousy, fits of anger, rivalries, dissensions, divisions, envy, drunkenness, orgies, and things like these. I warn you, as I warned you before, that those who do such things will not inherit the kingdom of God (Gal. 5:19-21).

Peter did the same:

---

[2] See my *Evangelicals Warned*; *Relationship*.

[3] It is also a nonsensical abomination; God frequently mocked it in the days of the old covenant. See, for instance, 1 Kings 18:26-27; Ps. 135:15-17; Isa. 44:9-20; Jer. 10:5. See also my 'Do You Get The Joke' (a discourse on Isa. 46:1-4) on my sermonaudio.com page. Idolatry – however it manifests itself – remains nonsense to this day.

The time that is past suffices for doing what the Gentiles want to do, living in sensuality, passions, drunkenness, orgies, drinking parties, and lawless idolatry (1 Pet. 4:3).

Ancient Greece, ancient Rome, heathen nations one and all, and – worst of the lot, the sophisticated West of the 21st century – idolaters, idolaters by nature and by choice, every man jack! Conversion could be described as the sinner turning from idolatry to the one true God. In the preaching of the gospel, God calls sinners to forsake idols. Take Paul and Barnabas who, when faced with idolatry-in-the-raw at Lystra, rebuked the pagans, telling them:

We bring you good news, that you should turn from these vain things [that is, idols][4] to a living God, who made the heaven and the earth and the sea and all that is in them (Acts 14:15).

In his sovereign grace, God, in Christ, has propitiated his wrath against his elect, and delivered them from the world and all its idolatrous corruption:

The Lord Jesus Christ... gave himself for our sins to deliver us from the present evil age, according to the will of our God and Father (Gal. 1:3-4).[5]

Do you not know that the unrighteous will not inherit the kingdom of God? Do not be deceived: neither the sexually immoral, nor idolaters, nor adulterers, nor men who practice homosexuality, nor thieves, nor the greedy, nor drunkards, nor revilers, nor swindlers will inherit the kingdom of God. And such were some of you. But you were washed, you were sanctified, you were justified in the name of the Lord Jesus Christ and by the Spirit of our God (1 Cor. 6:9-11).

[God] has rescued us from the dominion of darkness and brought us into the kingdom of the Son he loves (Col. 1:13).

You turned to God from idols to serve the living and true God, and to wait for his Son from heaven, whom he raised from the

---

[4] See Deut. 32:21; 1 Sam. 12:21; Jer. 8:19; 14:22; 1 Cor. 8:4.
[5] Rescued us from this world, this evil age, please note – not merely rescued us from damnation.

dead, Jesus who delivers us from the wrath to come (1 Thess. 1:9-10).

And believers, having been liberated from the idolatry of the world (John 8:4-36), are to keep themselves free of it:

> I wrote to you in my letter not to associate with sexually immoral people – not at all meaning the sexually immoral of this world, or the greedy and swindlers, or idolaters, since then you would need to go out of the world. But now I am writing to you not to associate with anyone who bears the name of brother if he is guilty of sexual immorality or greed, or is an idolater, reviler, drunkard, or swindler – not even to eat with such a one (1 Cor. 5:9-11).

> Do not be idolaters as some of [the Jews] were... Therefore, my beloved, flee from idolatry. I speak as to sensible people; judge for yourselves what I say. The cup of blessing that we bless, is it not a participation in the blood of Christ? The bread that we break, is it not a participation in the body of Christ? Because there is one bread, we who are many are one body, for we all partake of the one bread. Consider the people of Israel: are not those who eat the sacrifices participants in the altar? What do I imply then? That food offered to idols is anything, or that an idol is anything? No, I imply that what pagans sacrifice they offer to demons and not to God. I do not want you to be participants with demons. You cannot drink the cup of the Lord and the cup of demons. You cannot partake of the table of the Lord and the table of demons. Shall we provoke the Lord to jealousy? Are we stronger than he? (1 Cor. 10:7,14-22).

> Do not be unequally yoked with unbelievers. For what partnership has righteousness with lawlessness? Or what fellowship has light with darkness? What accord has Christ with Belial? Or what portion does a believer share with an unbeliever? What agreement has the temple of God with idols? For we are the temple of the living God; as God said: 'I will make my dwelling among them and walk among them, and I will be their God, and they shall be my people. Therefore go out from their midst, and be separate from them, says the Lord, and touch no unclean thing; then I will welcome you, and I will be a father to you, and you shall be sons and daughters to me, says the Lord Almighty' (2 Cor. 6:14-18).

Put to death... what is earthly in you: sexual immorality, impurity, passion, evil desire, and covetousness, which is idolatry. On account of these the wrath of God is coming. In these you too once walked, when you were living in them (Col. 3:5-7).

Little children, keep yourselves from idols (1 John 5:21).

The rest of mankind, who were not killed by these plagues, did not repent of the works of their hands nor give up worshipping demons and idols of gold and silver and bronze and stone and wood, which cannot see or hear or walk, nor did they repent of their murders or their sorceries or their sexual immorality or their thefts (Rev. 9:20-21).

The cowardly, the faithless, the detestable, as for murderers, the sexually immoral, sorcerers, idolaters, and all liars, their portion will be in the lake that burns with fire and sulphur, which is the second death (Rev. 21:8).

Concerning Babylon, the epitome of sin, the world, idolatry:

Come out of her, my people, lest you take part in her sins, lest you share in her plagues; for her sins are heaped high as heaven, and God has remembered her iniquities (Rev. 18:4-5).

In short:

Therefore, I urge you, brothers, in view of God's mercy, to offer your bodies as living sacrifices, holy and pleasing to God – this is your spiritual act of worship. Do not conform any longer to the pattern of this world, but be transformed by the renewing of your mind (Rom. 12:1-2).

Therefore be imitators of God, as beloved children. And walk in love, as Christ loved us and gave himself up for us, a fragrant offering and sacrifice to God.
But sexual immorality and all impurity or covetousness must not even be named among you, as is proper among saints. Let there be no filthiness nor foolish talk nor crude joking, which are out of place, but instead let there be thanksgiving. For you may be sure of this, that everyone who is sexually immoral or impure, or who is covetous (that is, an idolater), has no inheritance in the kingdom of Christ and God. Let no one deceive you with empty words, for because of these things the wrath of God comes upon the sons of disobedience. Therefore

do not become partners with them; for at one time you were darkness, but now you are light in the Lord. Walk as children of light (for the fruit of light is found in all that is good and right and true), and try to discern what is pleasing to the Lord. Take no part in the unfruitful works of darkness, but instead expose them. For it is shameful even to speak of the things that they do in secret. But when anything is exposed by the light, it becomes visible, for anything that becomes visible is light. Therefore it says: 'Awake, O sleeper, and arise from the dead, and Christ will shine on you'.

Look carefully then how you walk, not as unwise but as wise, making the best use of the time, because the days are evil. Therefore do not be foolish, but understand what the will of the Lord is. And do not get drunk with wine, for that is debauchery, but be filled with the Spirit, addressing one another in psalms and hymns and spiritual songs, singing and making melody to the Lord with your heart, giving thanks always and for everything to God the Father in the name of our Lord Jesus Christ, submitting to one another out of reverence for Christ (Eph. 5:1-20).

Jesus also suffered outside the gate in order to sanctify the people through his own blood. Therefore let us go to him outside the camp and bear the reproach he endured (Heb. 13:12-13).

Since this is what believers are, since this is what believers are required to be, at best they are always going to be suspect in the eyes of the world: believers are inevitable separatists, bound to and determined to keep themselves separate from the world – at least, they should be – and the world will not like it; the world demands conformity to its changing norms, but believers cannot and will not comply. God's people – of both covenants – are congenital misfits (old-covenant Israel by natural birth, new covenant Israel (Gal. 6:16; Phil. 3:3; 1 Pet. 2:9-10) by regeneration (2 Thess. 2:13; 1 Pet. 1:1-2), and, as an inevitable result, are persecuted: 'Has not my inheritance become to me like a speckled bird of prey that other birds of prey surround and attack?', asks God (Jer. 12:9).

I mentioned the 'changing norms' of idolatry. Take atheism. Because the first believers would have no truck with idolatry and pagan temples, the pagans accused them of atheism, and made them pay for it. How the tables have been turned! Who are the atheists today?[6]

And that is far from the worst of it from the world's point of view: it is not simply that believers insist on keeping themselves separate, but they will not shut up about it! Of course not! Believers are not to be passively separate from the world, silent about their rejection of paganism, their refusal and hatred of idolatry, but, in obedience to their Lord's command and commission, they are to go into all the world and preach the gospel (Matt. 28:18-20; Mark 16:15-16) in order that God may use them in his work of converting other sinners to Christ, delivering them from the world's evil, from Satan's grasp. This, it goes without saying, inevitably sets believers even more definitely on a collision course with the world. Satan does not calmly accept the loss of his slaves to Christ. Christ himself is unpalatable to the natural man, and his gospel meets the same hostility, as do his people when they confront pagans with Christ. The gospel is not a decent alternative in the eyes of the world; it is utterly objectionable. Saul of Tarsus, an eminent Jew, hated Christ and persecuted him in his people; as Christ told him: 'Saul, Saul, why are you persecuting me?... I am Jesus, whom you are persecuting' (Acts 9:4-5). He was set in the Caiaphas mode of wanting to annihilate Christ (John 11:47-53).[7]

It is easy to see why the world hates Christ. Christ is not just a Saviour, one Saviour among many – perhaps the best of the

---

[6] In the time of the first believers, 'any person who did not believe in any deity supported by the State was fair game to accusations of atheism... Early Christians were widely reviled as atheists because they did not believe in the existence of the Roman gods. During the Roman Empire, Christians were executed for their rejection of the pagan deities in general, and the Imperial cult of ancient Rome in particular' (Wikipedia).

[7] Remember also Matt. 25:31-46 – kindness shown or not shown to a fellow-believer is kindness shown or not shown to Christ himself. 'Whoever is generous to the poor lends to the LORD' (Prov. 19:17); 'Whoever receives you receives me' (Matt. 10:40).

bunch – but still just one of many. He is unique. It has to be trust in him and submission to him, and him alone; or else. He said so:

> I am the way, and the truth, and the life. No one comes to the Father except through me (John 14:6).

And so the first believers preached:

> Jesus Christ... there is salvation in no one else, for there is no other name under heaven given among men by which we must be saved (Acts 4:10-12).

> There is one God, and there is one mediator between God and men, the man Christ Jesus (1 Tim. 2:5).

It is in this spirit that believers have to confront the world and its culture with their unpalatable (as the world sees it) gospel. Christ did; the apostles did; and so must we. As Christ explained:

> Do you think that I have come to give peace on earth? No, I tell you, but rather division. For from now on in one house there will be five divided, three against two and two against three. They will be divided, father against son and son against father, mother against daughter and daughter against mother, mother-in-law against her daughter-in-law and daughter-in-law against mother-in-law (Luke 12:51-53).

And this has consequences:

> Do not think that I have come to bring peace to the earth. I have not come to bring peace, but a sword. For I have come to set a man against his father, and a daughter against her mother, and a daughter-in-law against her mother-in-law. And a person's enemies will be those of his own household. Whoever loves father or mother more than me is not worthy of me, and whoever loves son or daughter more than me is not worthy of me. And whoever does not take his cross and follow me is not worthy of me. Whoever finds his life will lose it, and whoever loses his life for my sake will find it (Matt. 10:34-39).

As Christ confronted sinners, so must believers:

> A servant is not greater than his master, nor is a messenger greater than the one who sent him (John 13:16).

And the world will not like it. It did not like it when Christ or the apostles challenged its culture; it will not like it when we do. Like it? The world hates it!

Let me prove it.

Christ had warned his disciples, doing so in the starkest and bluntest of terms: just as the world had hated him and his words, it would hate them and their words (John 15:18-27; 16:2-4,33; 17:14-18). Those believers knew that the world had hated the prophets for centuries past, and killed them (Matt. 23:31,34,37; Luke 11:47; 13:54; Rom. 11:3; 1 Thess. 2:15). They did not forget that the world (to put it mildly) had not welcomed Christ (John 1:11), but had hated him and wanted to kill him, even from birth (Matt. 2:1-20; Rev. 12:1-6), let alone when he began his ministry (Luke 4:28-29; John 5:18; 7:1,19; 8:37,40; 11:47-53,57). Eventually, they got their way. And now it would be the turn of believers; the world would hate them. They expected it. Christ could not have made the position clearer:

> Behold, I am sending you out as sheep in the midst of wolves, so be wise as serpents and innocent as doves. Beware of men, for they will deliver you over to courts and flog you in their synagogues, and you will be dragged before governors and kings for my sake, to bear witness before them and the Gentiles... Brother will deliver brother over to death, and the father his child, and children will rise against parents and have them put to death, and you will be hated by all for my name's sake (Matt. 10:16-22).

> They will deliver you up to tribulation and put you to death, and you will be hated by all nations for my name's sake (Matt. 24:9).

> If the world hates you, know that it has hated me before it hated you. If you were of the world, the world would love you as its own; but because you are not of the world, but I chose you out of the world, therefore the world hates you. Remember the word that I said to you: 'A servant is not greater than his master'. If they persecuted me, they will also persecute you. If they kept my word, they will also keep yours (John 15:18-20).

I have given them your word and the world has hated them, for they are not of the world any more than I am of the world. My prayer is not that you take them out of the world but that you protect them from the evil one. They are not of the world, even as I am not of it. Sanctify them by the truth; your word is truth. As you sent me into the world, I have sent them into the world (John 17:14-18).

As he told his half-brothers:

The world cannot hate you, but it hates me because I testify about it that its works are evil (John 7:7).

Oh yes, the early believers knew that what they were as believers, what they did as believers, what they stood for as believers, what they wanted by their preaching, and what and how they preached was going to be anathema to the world, the culture in which they were to live and evangelise. Naturally, at first, they thought only in terms of the Jews, but they soon learned what Christ had meant when he said they had to take the gospel into all the world. All the world! It meant, of course, that they would be confronted by, and have to confront, not only Jews, but pagans, principally (for a start) Greeks and Romans. If they were going to obey Christ, they knew that such confrontation was inevitable. They had no illusions about it. They knew that the world's hatred was an integral part of their stance for Christ; it 'went with the territory'. This hatred was not 'a difficulty' which took them by surprise; they had been forewarned about it, and, as expected, they experienced it. They did not go out of their way needlessly or gratuitously to court or provoke it,[8] but they knew it was the way God was going to advance the cause of Christ as they took the gospel to sinners. 'All who desire to live a godly life in Christ Jesus will be persecuted' (2 Tim. 3:12). Paul and Barnabas understood that 'strengthening the souls of the disciples, encouraging them to continue in the faith, and saying that through many tribulations we must enter the kingdom of God' (Acts 14:22) was a vital part

---

[8] Compare Jehovah's Witnesses. Knowing that martyrdom attracts, they have been more than willing to provoke opposition; take their stance on blood transfusions, for instance.

of their ministry. Believers knew that if they stayed faithful to Christ they would meet trouble. Had Christ not told them: 'Woe to you, when all people speak well of you, for so their fathers did to the false prophets' (Luke 6:26)?

Nevertheless, it wasn't long after Pentecost that believers were being tempted to compromise with the cultures around them.[9] But the apostles stepped in, disabused them, instructing them as to what was required of them in their approach to hostile cultures. Take Paul. As he made clear when writing to the Corinthians:

> The word of the cross is folly to those who are perishing, but to us who are being saved it is the power of God. For it is written: 'I will destroy the wisdom of the wise, and the discernment of the discerning I will thwart'. Where is the one who is wise? Where is the scribe? Where is the debater of this age? Has not God made foolish the wisdom of the world? For since, in the wisdom of God, the world did not know God through wisdom, it pleased God through the folly of what we preach to save those who believe. For Jews demand signs and Greeks seek wisdom, but we preach Christ crucified, a stumbling block to Jews and folly to Gentiles, but to those who are called, both Jews and Greeks, Christ the power of God and the wisdom of God. For the foolishness of God is wiser than men, and the weakness of God is stronger than men...
> And I, when I came to you, brothers, did not come proclaiming to you the testimony of God with lofty speech or wisdom. For I decided [or determined] to know nothing among you except Jesus Christ and him crucified. And I was with you in weakness and in fear and much trembling, and my speech and my message were not in plausible words of wisdom, but in demonstration of the Spirit and of power, so that your faith might not rest in the wisdom of men but in the power of God. Yet among the mature we do impart wisdom, although it is not a wisdom of this age or of the rulers of this age, who are

---

[9] Rome has been doing it 'successfully' for 1500 years; evangelicals, I fear, are rapidly becoming expert in using pagan culture, as they imagine, to advance the gospel. See my *Relationship*. Evangelicals might think they can control pagans; paganism, I am convinced, will prove them mistaken.

doomed to pass away. But we impart a secret and hidden wisdom of God, which God decreed before the ages for our glory. None of the rulers of this age understood this, for if they had, they would not have crucified the Lord of glory...
Let no one deceive himself. If anyone among you thinks that he is wise in this age, let him become a fool that he may become wise. For the wisdom of this world is folly with God. For it is written: 'He catches the wise in their craftiness'; and again: 'The Lord knows the thoughts of the wise, that they are futile'. So let no one boast in men (1 Cor. 1:18-25; 2:1-8; 3:18-21).

I beg of you that when I am present I may not have to show boldness with such confidence as I count on showing against some who suspect us of walking according to the flesh. For though we walk in the flesh, we are not waging war according to the flesh. For the weapons of our warfare are not of the flesh but have divine power to destroy strongholds. We destroy arguments and every lofty opinion raised against the knowledge of God, and take every thought captive to obey Christ, being ready to punish every disobedience, when your obedience is complete (2 Cor. 10:2-6).

Yes, confrontation with the surrounding cultures was bound to be the experience of the early *ekklēsia*. There was no way of avoiding it and staying loyal to the gospel.

This confrontation, of course, did not come from a spirit of bravado. Paul certainly felt his weakness in preaching the gospel, his flesh tightened at the thought of pain, and he was not ashamed to confess it. As we have just seen, as he told the Corinthians:

I was with you in weakness and in fear and much trembling (1 Cor. 2:2).

No *braggadocio* here![10] As he pleaded with the believers at Ephesus:

[Pray] for me, that words may be given to me in opening my mouth boldly to proclaim the mystery of the gospel, for which I

---

[10] For more on Paul's sense of weakness, see 1 Cor. 4:10; 2 Cor. 11:30; 12:5,9ff.; 13:9.

am an ambassador in chains, that I may declare it boldly, as I ought to speak (Eph. 6:19-20).

Pray also for us, that God may open to us a door for the word, to declare the mystery of Christ, on account of which I am in prison – that I may make it clear, which is how I ought to speak (Col. 4:3-4).

Despite his fear, he did not run away from confronting the world and its cultures. While this following extract comes from his letter to the believers at Rome, it surely gives a strong indication of how Paul preached to pagans – I am referring to his classic statement about the cause and inevitable effect of idolatry:

The wrath of God is revealed from heaven against all ungodliness and unrighteousness of men, who by their unrighteousness suppress the truth. For what can be known about God is plain to them, because God has shown it to them. For his invisible attributes, namely, his eternal power and divine nature, have been clearly perceived, ever since the creation of the world, in the things that have been made. So they are without excuse. For although they knew God, they did not honour him as God or give thanks to him, but they became futile in their thinking, and their foolish hearts were darkened. Claiming to be wise, they became fools, and exchanged the glory of the immortal God for images resembling mortal man and birds and animals and creeping things... They exchanged the truth about God for a lie and worshipped and served the creature rather than the Creator, who is blessed forever! Amen... They did not see fit to acknowledge God (Rom. 1:18-23,25,28).

In taking such a stance, Paul was not courting popularity was he? Was he not walking in the steps of his Master? Remember how he had confronted his hearers (Matt. 11:21-24; John 8:31-47, for instance).[11] As for Paul, when writing to the Galatians, he was explicit about it:

Am I... seeking the approval of man, or of God? Or am I trying to please man? If I were still trying to please man, I would not be a servant of Christ (Gal. 1:10).

---

[11] See my *In Church or In Christ*.

As he was when addressing the Thessalonians:

> Though we had already suffered and been shamefully treated at Philippi, as you know, we had boldness in our God to declare to you the gospel of God in the midst of much conflict. For our appeal does not spring from error or impurity or any attempt to deceive, but just as we have been approved by God to be entrusted with the gospel, so we speak, not to please man, but to please God who tests our hearts. For we never came with words of flattery, as you know, nor with a pretext for greed – God is witness. Nor did we seek glory from people, whether from you or from others, though we could have made demands as apostles of Christ (1 Thess. 2:2-6).

Again:

> For you, brothers, became imitators of the churches of God in Christ Jesus that are in Judea. For you suffered the same things from your own countrymen as they did from the Jews, who killed both the Lord Jesus and the prophets, and drove us out, and displease God and oppose all mankind by hindering us from speaking to the Gentiles that they might be saved (1 Thess. 2:14-16).

And the apostle, being deeply anxious about their resolve, sent Timothy to find out how they were standing up to it:

> Therefore when we could bear it no longer, we were willing to be left behind at Athens alone, and we sent Timothy, our brother and God's co-worker in the gospel of Christ, to establish and exhort you in your faith, that no one be moved by these afflictions. For you yourselves know that we are destined for this. For when we were with you, we kept telling you beforehand that we were to suffer affliction, just as it has come to pass, and just as you know. For this reason, when I could bear it no longer, I sent to learn about your faith, for fear that somehow the tempter had tempted you and our labour would be in vain (1 Thess. 3:1-5).

Idolatry – whatever form it takes – is always the ethos of the culture which surrounds believers, and tries to engulf them; indeed, they themselves were once caught up in that evil world, but by God's sovereign grace they have been regenerated, converted and delivered from it:

The Lord Jesus Christ... gave himself for our sins to deliver us from the present evil age, according to the will of our God and Father (Gal. 1:3-4).

You were dead in the trespasses and sins in which you once walked, following the course of this world [or age], following the prince of the power of the air, the spirit that is now at work in the sons of disobedience – among whom we all once lived in the passions of our flesh, carrying out the desires of the body and the mind, and were by nature children of wrath, like the rest of mankind. But God, being rich in mercy, because of the great love with which he loved us, even when we were dead in our trespasses, made us alive together with Christ – by grace you have been saved – and raised us up with him and seated us with him in the heavenly places in Christ Jesus, so that in the coming ages he might show the immeasurable riches of his grace in kindness toward us in Christ Jesus. For by grace you have been saved through faith... (Eph. 2:1-8).

And believers have constantly to resist the temptation to return to that old culture, not least in their thinking and in their heart. As for Jewish converts, the old covenant could beckon – hence the letter to the Hebrews. As for Gentile converts, the old pagan way could still seem attractive. The apostles knew it and measured up to it, not with sugar and soft soap, but hard-nosed reality and blunt command:

Do not be conformed to this world [or age or culture], but be transformed by the renewal of your mind (Rom. 12:2).

Since therefore Christ suffered in the flesh [that is, died], arm yourselves with the same way of thinking, for whoever has suffered in the flesh [that is, died] has ceased from sin, so as to live for the rest of the time in the flesh no longer for human passions but for the will of God. For the time that is past suffices for doing what the Gentiles want to do, living in sensuality, passions, drunkenness, orgies, drinking parties, and lawless idolatry. With respect to this they are surprised when you do not join them in the same flood of debauchery, and they malign you; but they will give account to him who is ready to judge the living and the dead (1 Pet. 4:1-5).[12]

---

[12] As Paul told the Roman believers: 'Each of us will give an account of himself to God' (Rom. 14:12; see also Matt. 12:36; 16:27).

Do not love the world or the things in the world. If anyone loves the world, the love of the Father is not in him. For all that is in the world – the desires of the flesh and the desires of the eyes and pride of life – is not from the Father but is from the world. And the world is passing away along with its desires, but whoever does the will of God abides forever (1 John 2:15-17).

Such was the life of the early believers.

* * *

What has all this to do with the resurrection and the kingdom? If I may accommodate the apostle's words: 'Much in every way' (Rom. 3:2).

Before coming to the resurrection, let me make a general point. The gospel, if it is preached as it ought to be preached – including, of course, the proclamation of its proper, personal consequences – will always offend the natural man. Take creation. The very mention of creation is a red rag to the world; it is not merely a question of 'science'; at bottom, it is a question of authority, Godship. The children of the world cannot let God be God; they will not let him be God; they will not acknowledge their obligation to him, and – above all – their accountability to him. And that is why the professors of atheism are so militant in their attacks upon biblical creationism and its proponents. Something similar can be said about God's predestinating power, the fall of man, God's sovereignty in regeneration, the necessity of redemption, and so on. Above all, it is the preaching of Christ – Christ, his person and work – which the world cannot abide; it 'hate[s] him', and naturally 'We do not want this man to reign over us' is its chorus (Luke 19:14).

Natural men are idolaters – any god will do as long as he is not the God revealed in the Bible, the God and Father of our Lord Jesus Christ. This is the crux of the battle in which believers are always engaged, always – in every generation. And it comes to a head whenever the resurrection and the kingdom, and the consequences of both, are raised and pressed home. The first believers certainly found it so when they proclaimed Christ's resurrection.

When writing to the Romans, having set out the appalling condition of the natural man as a wilful and stubborn idolater, in order to highlight the contrast between the unbeliever – one who refuses to allow (or, at the very least, will not acknowledge) that God has the power to create, to give life – and the believer – one who is convinced that God can do the seeming impossible, can work miracles – Paul turned to Abraham. And what a contrast! Abraham certainly trusted God to perform what he had promised and accomplish for him the ostensibly unattainable:

> The promise to Abraham and his offspring that he would be heir of the world did not come through the law but through the righteousness of faith. For if it is the adherents of the law who are to be the heirs, faith is null and the promise is void. For the law brings wrath, but where there is no law there is no transgression.
> That is why it depends on faith, in order that the promise may rest on grace and be guaranteed to all his offspring – not only to the adherent of the law but also to the one who shares the faith of Abraham, who is the father of us [that is, believers] all, as it is written: 'I have made you the father of many nations' – in the presence of the God in whom he believed, who gives life to the dead and calls into existence the things that do not exist.
> In hope [Abraham] believed against hope, that he should become the father of many nations, as he had been told: 'So shall your offspring be'. He did not weaken in faith when he considered his own body, which was as good as dead (since he was about a hundred years old), or when he considered the barrenness of Sarah's womb. No unbelief made him waver concerning the promise of God, but he grew strong in his faith as he gave glory to God, fully convinced that God was able to do what he had promised (Rom. 4:13-21).

Moreover, did Abraham not show his confidence in God's power to raise the dead when he was prepared to sacrifice his son (Gen. 22:1-18)? The writer to the Hebrews spelled it out:

> By faith Abraham, when he was tested, offered up Isaac, and he who had received the promises was in the act of offering up his only son, of whom it was said: 'Through Isaac shall your

offspring be named'. He considered that God was able even to raise him from the dead, from which, figuratively speaking, he did receive him back (Heb. 11:17-19).

As N.T.Wright observed, the point is:

> Faith in the resurrection power of God, according to Paul, is the alternative to idolatry; it assigns to the creator God the power and the glory which are properly his, the very things that idolatry characteristically denies, and by denying courts death. [This is too weak; the natural man, from birth, is under the wrath of God, and is dead in sin, and is on the road to eternal death (John 3:18,36; Rom. 1:18; Eph. 2:1-3) – DG].[13]

My concern here – as was for the first believers – is with the resurrection of Christ: not merely the fact of the resurrection – a miracle which the world will not allow, cannot allow, a miracle which the world scoffs at and ridicules – but the weight, the consequences, the connotations which Christ's resurrection inevitably carries; namely, that Christ is the true and only King, that he has a kingdom, and that kingdom is everlasting, and that death could not hold him back from coming into that kingdom. Men might hate him and do all they can to thwart him and his rule, but they are doomed to fail; they crucified him and he was buried, but he rose from the dead. To preach, to proclaim, the risen Christ, therefore, means that believers inevitably find themselves in confrontation – indeed, colliding – with the world on these issues. Moreover, the first believers knew they had to confront the world on these matters. It is the same for us, today. The world insists on having its own king, its own kingdom. So when Christ – raised and King – is preached, the world will fight back with every weapon at its disposal.

---

[13] Wright p735. While Wright was right to point out that 'we must not' reduce the resurrection by simply 'saying that Jesus' crucifixion had been a victory rather than a defeat', and thinking of it only as 'my sins have been forgiven' (Wright p728; see also Wright pp730,735), it does include both. I have tackled Wright on personal conversion before – see my *Hinge*; *Conversion*. We do not preach Christianity; we preach Christ.

This is what the first believers found, but they did not shirk it. C.S.Lewis:

> To preach the gospel[14] meant (to the apostles) primarily to preach the resurrection... The resurrection is the central theme in every Christian sermon reported in the Acts. The resurrection, and its consequences, were the 'gospel' or good news which the Christians brought.[15]

Yet this would have been regarded as anything but 'good news' by most listeners. Take the Jews. As Wright explained:

> The resurrection... set the early Christians on a course of confrontation, not to say collision, with other Jewish groups of their day, particularly the authorities. Any claim that Israel's God[16] had acted *here* rather than somewhere else in Judaism (the temple, for example! [see Acts 7 – DG]) and in *this* way vindicating a man whose work and teaching had been highly controversial [too weak: Christ's work, teaching and person had been overwhelmingly loathed by the Jewish authorities; so much so, they realised that to preserve their status, not to say save their skin, he had to be got rid of (see John 11:45-53) – DG], was bound to create a storm, and soon it did. Hard-line Pharisees like Saul of Tarsus, bent on a very different eschatological [prophetical] and political agenda, were horrified at the talk that *this* man being raised from the dead, with all that it implied. The official hierarchy, mostly Sadducees, were doubly horrified. Resurrection always had been a novel, revolutionary doctrine, and this new movement proved their worst fears about it to be true.[17]

Just so! Luke has carefully recorded the history of this early confrontation.

But before I look at that record, a glance back to the way in which talk of the resurrection brought conflict for Christ himself:

---

[14] Lewis had 'Christianity'.
[15] C.S.Lewis: *Miracles.*
[16] Wright used lower-case 'g'.
[17] Wright p727, emphasis original.

The Jews said to [Christ]: 'What sign do you show us for doing these things?' Jesus answered them: 'Destroy this temple, and in three days I will raise it up'. The Jews then said: 'It has taken forty-six years to build this temple, and will you raise it up in three days?'' But he was speaking about the temple of his body. When therefore he was raised from the dead, his disciples remembered that he had said this, and they believed the Scripture and the word that Jesus had spoken (John 2:18-22).

'For this reason the Father loves me, because I lay down my life that I may take it up again. No one takes it from me, but I lay it down of my own accord. I have authority to lay it down, and I have authority to take it up again. This charge I have received from my Father'. There was again a division among the Jews because of these words. Many of them said: 'He has a demon, and is insane; why listen to him?' Others said: 'These are not the words of one who is oppressed by a demon. Can a demon open the eyes of the blind?' (John 10:17-21).

Yes, Christ certainly collided with the Jews over the question of his resurrection. Now for the post-Pentecost experience of the first believers.

Let me start my look at Acts by picking up the narrative just a little way into the account:

The captain of the temple and the Sadducees came upon [Peter and John], greatly annoyed because they were teaching the people and proclaiming in ['in the case of' – NASB margin] Jesus the resurrection from the dead (Acts 4:1-2).

'Greatly annoyed'? What a weak translation of the Greek! They were grieved, exasperated, sore troubled, offended, pained, greatly disturbed; not to put too fine a point in it, the temple officials and the Sadducees were livid, up in arms, worked up about it. About what? About the believers preaching Christ and his resurrection, with all its consequences (see also Acts 2:24,32; 3:15,26; 4:10; 5:30; 10:40; 13:30-37; 17:18,31-32).

The Jews hated the thought that God, by raising Jesus from the dead, had exposed them as fools by utterly ruining their scheme to use the Romans to destroy, once and forever, this (as they saw him) upstart-Messiah (Matt. 26:3-5; John 11:47-53), the rabble-rouser, and that the believers were now actually preaching this resurrected Jesus as the Christ, the Messiah! Things could not have turned out worse! The Sadducees – the top dogs in Judaism at this time – were even more incensed than the rest of the Jews because they refused to believe in any resurrection whatsoever! Clearly, if the believers persisted in preaching Christ risen from the dead, the early *ekklēsia* was certain to clash with the Jews, and clash violently. The first believers, however, did not hesitate, they did not flinch, they did not shy away from this conflict. Quite the opposite! They did not mute the resurrection. Oh no! They deliberately preached – proclaimed – the risen Christ, deliberately confronted the Jews over the issue, and at every turn,[18] and did so right from the word 'Go' – the day of Pentecost – laying the blame for Christ's death fairly and squarely on those responsible for it. Even in his opening remarks in that first public proclamation of the age of the new covenant, Peter went for the jugular:

> Men of Israel, hear these words: Jesus of Nazareth, a man attested to you by God with mighty works and wonders and signs that God did through him in your midst, as you yourselves know – this Jesus, delivered up according to the definite plan and foreknowledge of God, you crucified and killed by the hands of lawless men [that is, Gentiles]. God raised him up, loosing the pangs of death, because it was not possible for him to be held by it (Acts 2:22-24).

Not only that! He confronted the Jews with the fact that the Old Testament – their very own Scriptures – in particular, David in Psalm 16:8-11 – had foretold them of it. Moreover, he – Peter (whom they dismissed as utterly ignorant – see Acts 4:13) – was now having the audacity to confront them even further by (as they would see it) teaching his Jewish grandfathers to suck eggs:

> Brothers, I may say to you with confidence about the patriarch David that he both died and was buried, and his tomb is with us to this day. Being therefore a prophet, and knowing that God

---

[18] Very much as Jesus himself had confronted the Jews over the sabbath (to take just one Gospel, see John chapters 5, 7 and 9).

had sworn with an oath to him that he would set one of his descendants on his throne, he foresaw and spoke about the resurrection of the Christ, that he was not abandoned to Hades, nor did his flesh see corruption. This Jesus God raised up, and of that we all are witnesses. Being therefore exalted at the right hand of God, and having received from the Father the promise of the Holy Spirit, he has poured out this that you yourselves are seeing and hearing. For David did not ascend into the heavens, but he himself says: 'The Lord said to my Lord: "Sit at my right hand, until I make your enemies your footstool"'. Let all the house of Israel therefore know for certain that God has made him both Lord and Christ, this Jesus whom you crucified (Acts 2:29-36).

Phew!

The dust had hardly settled on this confrontation when Peter (accompanied by John) added insult to injury (in the eyes of the Jewish leaders) by what he said in his discourse to the gathered crowd following the cure of lame man at the Beautiful Gate:

Men of Israel, why do you wonder at this, or why do you stare at us, as though by our own power or piety we have made him walk? The God of Abraham, the God of Isaac, and the God of Jacob, the God of our fathers, glorified his servant Jesus, whom you delivered over and denied in the presence of Pilate, when he had decided to release him. But you denied the Holy and Righteous One, and asked for a murderer to be granted to you, and you killed the Author of life, whom God raised from the dead. To this we are witnesses. And his name – by faith in his name – has made this man strong whom you see and know, and the faith that is through Jesus has given the man this perfect health in the presence of you all.

And now, brothers, I know that you acted in ignorance, as did also your rulers. But what God foretold by the mouth of all the prophets, that his Christ would suffer, he thus fulfilled. Repent therefore, and turn back, that your sins may be blotted out, that times of refreshing may come from the presence of the Lord, and that he may send the Christ appointed for you, Jesus, whom heaven must receive until the time for restoring all the things about which God spoke by the mouth of his holy prophets long ago. Moses said: 'The Lord God will raise up for you a prophet like me from your brothers. You shall listen to him in whatever he tells you. And it shall be that every soul who does not listen to that prophet shall be destroyed from the people'. And all the prophets who have spoken, from Samuel and those who came after him, also proclaimed these days. You are the sons of the prophets and of the covenant that God made with your fathers, saying to Abraham: 'And in your offspring shall all the families of the earth be blessed'. God, having raised up his servant, sent him to you first, to bless you by turning every one of you from your wickedness' (Acts 3:12-26).

This was the last straw! The authorities had had more than enough. They pounced:

> As [Peter and John] were speaking to the people, the priests and the captain of the temple and the Sadducees came upon them, greatly annoyed because they were teaching the people and proclaiming in Jesus the resurrection from the dead. And they arrested them and put them in custody until the next day, for it was already evening (Acts 4:1-3).

Even so, when the apostles were hauled before the court, Peter pulled no punches:

> Rulers of the people and elders, if we are being examined today concerning a good deed done to a crippled man, by what means this man has been healed, let it be known to all of you and to all the people of Israel that by the name of Jesus Christ of Nazareth, whom you crucified, whom God raised from the dead – by him this man is standing before you well. This Jesus is the stone that was rejected by you, the builders, which has become the cornerstone [quoting Ps. 118:22 to the religious leaders!]. And there is salvation in no one else, for there is no other name under heaven given among men by which we must be saved (Acts 4:8-12).

The leaders were appalled; they could not believe their ears:

> When they saw the boldness of Peter and John, and perceived that they were uneducated, common men, they were astonished (Acts 4:13).[19]

---

[19] Jamieson-Fausset-Brown commented: "'We thought we had got rid of him [that is, Jesus]; but lo! he reappears in these men, and all that troubled us in the Nazarene himself has yet to be put down in these his

Not only were the leaders appalled; they tried to put a stop to the apostles' preaching by the use of threats. Peter and John would have none of it:

> Whether it is right in the sight of God to listen to you rather than to God, you must judge, for we cannot but speak of what we have seen and heard (Acts 4:19-20).

Following which, they went back to their friends and, in light of Exodus 20; Nehemiah 9:6; Ps. 2:1; 146:6, prayed for courage to go on boldly proclaiming the risen Christ (Acts 4:23-31). God immediately answered, bestowing the Spirit upon them in an effusion of power: 'They were all filled with the Holy Spirit and continued to speak the word of God with boldness' (Acts 4:31).

The Jews did not take this lying down. In response to the apostles' refusal to be cowed, the Jewish authorities struck again:

> They [the bigwigs] set them [the apostles] before the council. And the high priest questioned them, saying: 'We strictly charged you not to teach in this name, yet here you have filled Jerusalem with your teaching, and you intend to bring this man's blood upon us'. But Peter and the apostles answered: 'We must obey God rather than men. The God of our fathers raised Jesus, whom you killed by hanging him on a tree. God exalted him at his right hand as Leader and Saviour, to give repentance to Israel and forgiveness of sins. And we are witnesses to these things, and so is the Holy Spirit, whom God has given to those who obey him' (Acts 5:27-32).

After some debate, the authorities:

> ...called in the apostles... beat them and charged them not to speak in the name of Jesus, and let them go (Acts 5:40).

So:

> Then [the apostles] left the presence of the council, rejoicing that they were counted worthy to suffer dishonour for the name. And every day, in the temple and from house to house,

---

disciples". What a testimony to these primitive [early] witnesses! Would that the same could be said of [us] their successors!'

they did not cease teaching and preaching that the Christ is Jesus (Acts 5:41-42).

Indeed, the message of the resurrection – and the conflict it caused – spread to Jews far beyond Jerusalem and wider Judea.

Paul and Barnabas, for instance, took up the spiritual cudgels when addressing the Jews in Pisidian Antioch:

Brothers, sons of the family of Abraham, and those among you who fear God [that is, proselytes], to us has been sent the message of this salvation. For those who live in Jerusalem and their rulers, because they did not recognise him [that is, Jesus] nor understand the utterances of the prophets, which are read every sabbath, fulfilled them by condemning him. And though they found in him no guilt worthy of death, they asked Pilate to have him executed. And when they had carried out all that was written of him, they took him down from the tree and laid him in a tomb. But God raised him from the dead, and for many days he appeared to those who had come up with him from Galilee to Jerusalem, who are now his witnesses to the people. And we bring you the good news that what God promised to the fathers, this he has fulfilled to us their children by raising Jesus, as also it is written in the second Psalm: 'You are my Son, today I have begotten you'. And as for the fact that he raised him from the dead, no more to return to corruption, he has spoken in this way: "I will give you the holy and sure blessings of David'. Therefore he says also in another psalm: 'You will not let your Holy One see corruption'. For David, after he had served the purpose of God in his own generation, fell asleep and was laid with his fathers and saw corruption, but he whom God raised up did not see corruption. Let it be known to you therefore, brothers, that through this man forgiveness of sins is proclaimed to you, and by him everyone who believes is freed [that is justified] from everything from which you could not be freed by the law of Moses. Beware, therefore, lest what is said in the prophets should come about: 'Look, you scoffers, be astounded and perish; for I am doing a work in your days, a work that you will not believe, even if one tells it to you' (Acts 13:26-41).

Then Paul and Silas:

...came to Thessalonica, where there was a synagogue of the Jews. And Paul went in, as was his custom, and on three sabbath days he reasoned with them from the Scriptures, explaining and proving that it was necessary for the Christ to suffer and to rise from the dead, and saying: 'This Jesus, whom I proclaim to you, is the Christ' (Acts 17:1-3).

The Jews, infuriated by such preaching, gathered and stirred up a rabble who hauled Paul and Silas before the authorities, laying this charge against them:

These men who have turned the world upside down have come here also, and Jason has received them, and they are all acting against the decrees of Caesar, saying that there is another king, Jesus. And the people and the city authorities were disturbed when they heard these things (Acts 17:6-8).

At Ephesus, Paul:

...entered the synagogue and for three months spoke boldly, reasoning and persuading them about the kingdom of God (Acts 19:8).

As he later told the Ephesian elders, when meeting them at Miletus, although he knew that imprisonment and worse awaited him at Jerusalem, he was determined to go there:

...if only I may finish my course and the ministry that I received from the Lord Jesus, to testify to the gospel of the grace of God. And now, behold, I know that none of you among whom I have gone about proclaiming the kingdom will see my face again. Therefore I testify to you this day that I am innocent of the blood of all, for I did not shrink from declaring to you the whole counsel of God (Acts 20:24-27).

And when he was under house arrest in Rome, he called the Jewish leaders to meet him:

When they had appointed a day for him, they came to him at his lodging in greater numbers. From morning till evening he expounded to them, testifying to the kingdom of God and trying to convince them about Jesus both from the law of Moses and from the prophets (Acts 28:23).

Although some of the leaders were convinced, others would have none of it. As they left, Paul quoted Isaiah 6:9-10 to them. He did not change his tune, or tone down the strain:

> He lived there two whole years at his own expense, and welcomed all who came to him, proclaiming the kingdom of God and teaching about the Lord Jesus Christ with all boldness and without hindrance (Acts 28:30-31).

So much for the Jews. Now for the pagans.

Take Samaria, the people who were a hybrid semi-pagan, semi-Jew:

> Philip went down to the city of Samaria and proclaimed to them the Christ... When they believed Philip as he preached good news about the kingdom of God and the name of Jesus Christ, they were baptised, both men and women (Acts 8:5,12).

Then we have the epoch-making move of the gospel being taken to the Gentiles with Peter addressing Cornelius and those gathered in the centurion's house:

> Truly I understand that God shows no partiality, but in every nation anyone who fears him and does what is right is acceptable to him. As for the word that he sent to Israel, preaching good news of peace through Jesus Christ (he is Lord of all), you yourselves know what happened throughout all Judea, beginning from Galilee after the baptism that John proclaimed: how God anointed Jesus of Nazareth with the Holy Spirit and with power. He went about doing good and healing all who were oppressed by the devil, for God was with him. And we are witnesses of all that he did both in the country of the Jews and in Jerusalem. They put him to death by hanging him on a tree, but God raised him on the third day and made him to appear, not to all the people but to us who had been chosen by God as witnesses, who ate and drank with him after he rose from the dead. And he commanded us to preach to the people and to testify that he is the one appointed by God to be judge of the living and the dead. To him all the prophets bear witness that everyone who believes in him receives forgiveness of sins through his name (Acts 10:34-43).

And when Paul was at Athens, facing the superstitious, religiously-besotted academics in the Areopagus, he dismissed their idolatry, declaring:

> We ought not to think that the divine being is like gold or silver or stone, an image formed by the art and imagination of man. The times of ignorance God overlooked, but now he commands all people everywhere to repent, because he has fixed a day on which he will judge the world in righteousness by a man whom he has appointed; and of this he has given assurance to all by raising him from the dead (Acts 17:29-31).[20]

His hearers responded:

> Now when they heard of the resurrection of the dead, some mocked. But others... (Acts 17:32).

Paul before Felix:

> This I confess to you, that according to the Way, which they call a sect, I worship the God of our fathers, believing everything laid down by the law and written in the prophets, having a hope in God, which these men themselves accept, that there will be a resurrection of both the just and the unjust... Some Jews from Asia – they ought to be here before you and to make an accusation, should they have anything against me. Or else let these men themselves say what wrongdoing they found when I stood before the council, other than this one thing that I cried out while standing among them: 'It is with respect to the resurrection of the dead that I am on trial before you this day' (Acts 24:14-21).

Felix listened to Paul again, and 'as [Paul] reasoned about righteousness and self-control and the coming judgment [following the return of Christ in power, of course], Felix was alarmed' (Acts 24:25).

Festus, seeking the help of Agrippa in the legal aspects of Paul's case, had explained by telling him that the Jews, in accusing Paul, had complained 'about a certain Jesus, who was dead, but whom Paul asserted to be alive' (Acts 25:19). When he stood before the king, the apostle went into detail:

---

[20] See my *To Confront*.

I stand here on trial because of my hope in the promise made by God to our fathers, to which our twelve tribes hope to attain, as they earnestly worship night and day. And for this hope I am accused by Jews, O king! Why is it thought incredible by any of you that God raises the dead?... To this day I have had the help that comes from God, and so I stand here testifying both to small and great, saying nothing but what the prophets and Moses said would come to pass: that the Christ must suffer and that, by being the first to rise from the dead, he would proclaim light both to our people and to the Gentiles (Acts 26:6-8,22-23).

And in Paul's closing retort, he returned to the prophets, making a pointed, rhetorical demand of Agrippa, and, without waiting for his reply, replied for him:

King Agrippa, do you believe the prophets? I know that you believe [them] (Acts 26:27).

The case is surely made: the kernel of the clash between the early believers and the cultures which surrounded them was Christ – the Messiah – the Son of God, Christ raised from the dead, Christ as King of his own kingdom, and as judge, and all as prophesied in the Old Testament. This is what the believers preached; and this is what so greatly aroused the wrath of the cultures – Christ raised, Christ the King.

Let me probe it further.

As for the Jews, as Wright put it:

The Sadducees were right to regard the doctrine of resurrection, and especially its announcement in relation to Jesus, as political dynamite.[21]

For Rome, Caesar was king, the only king; indeed, in the Roman world – that military and political power which dominated virtually all the known world at the time, including Jewry – the Emperor had to be worshipped – or, at the very least, publicly acknowledged – as divine: he had become a god. As we have seen, the Jews knew this was the most sensitive

---

[21] Wright p730.

point for Pilate – and, when they were blackmailing him to give into their demands and crucify Christ, they had no qualms about pressing it home:

> Pilate sought to release [Jesus], but the Jews cried out: 'If you release this man, you are not Caesar's friend. Everyone who makes himself a king opposes Caesar'. So when Pilate heard these words, he brought Jesus out and sat down on the judgment seat at a place called The Stone Pavement, and in Aramaic Gabbatha. Now it was the day of Preparation of the Passover. It was about the sixth hour. He said to the Jews: 'Behold your King!' They cried out: 'Away with him, away with him, crucify him!' Pilate said to them: 'Shall I crucify your King?' The chief priests answered: 'We have no king but Caesar'. So he delivered him over to them to be crucified (John 19:12-16).

Even so, Pilate made sure that he had the last word and got his own back on the Jews:

> Pilate also wrote an inscription and put it on the cross. It read: 'Jesus of Nazareth, the King of the Jews'. Many of the Jews read this inscription, for the place where Jesus was crucified was near the city, and it was written in Aramaic, in Latin, and in Greek. So the chief priests of the Jews said to Pilate: 'Do not write: "The King of the Jews", but rather: "This man said, I am King of the Jews". Pilate answered: 'What I have written I have written' (John 19:19-22).

Nigel Pollard explained the background Roman-thinking:

> [An] element in the Roman state-religion was what is generally referred to as the imperial cult. This cult regarded emperors and members of their families as gods.
> On his death, Julius Caesar was officially recognised as a god, the Divine ('Divus') Julius, by the Roman state. And in 29 BC Caesar's adopted son, the first Roman emperor Augustus, allowed the culturally Greek cities of Asia Minor to set up temples to him. This was really the first manifestation of Roman emperor-worship.
> While worship of a living emperor was culturally acceptable in some parts of the empire, in Rome itself and in Italy it was not. There an emperor was usually declared a 'divus' only on his death, and was subsequently worshipped (especially on

anniversaries, like that of his accession) with sacrifice like any other gods.[22]

Warren Carter:

The worship of emperors practiced in the towns and cities of the Roman Empire resembled ruler-worship elsewhere in the ancient world. The repertoire of activities was typical of religious practices in the classical world and included variously temples, shrines, altars, images, sacrifices, priests, processions, feasts, oaths of loyalty and obedience, hymns, poems, prayers, incense, and contests in athletics, music, and imperial encomiums. Expressions of worship could take place in households, trade associations, and in municipal, provincial, and state festivals.[23]

Wright:

There can be no question that the title ['son of god' – let alone 'Son of God' – DG] would have been heard by many in the Graeco-Roman world... as a challenge to Caesar.[24]

As we have seen, the first believers did not shirk this confrontation; there would be no compromise, even though it put them on the high road to possible execution.

Wright again:

Calling Jesus 'son of god' [let alone 'Son of God' – DG]... constituted a refusal to retreat, a determination to stop Christian discipleship turning into a private cult, a sect, a mystery religion. It launched a claim on the world: a claim at once absolute (a tiny group of nobodies cocking a snook at the might of Rome) and very serious, so serious that within a couple of generations the might of Rome was trying, and failing, to stamp it out... [The believers] refused to relinquish the world to the principalities and powers, but claimed even them for

---

[22] Nigel Pollard: 'The Imperial Cult', BBC website.

[23] Warren Carter: 'Imperial Cult and Early Christianity', *Oxford Bibliographies*, OUP website.

[24] Wright p729. Hence the centurion's remarkable statement at the cross following the death of Christ – with or without definite article and the upper case: 'Truly this man was the Son of God!' (Mark 15:39).

allegiance to the Messiah who was now the Lord, the *kurios*...
The resurrection of Jesus... supplies the groundwork for this...
[Believers] calling Jesus 'son of God' [let alone 'Son of God' –
DG]... constituted themselves by implication as a collection of
rebel cells within Caesar's empire, loyal to a different
monarch, a different *kurios* [Lord]... The Sadducees were right
to regard the doctrine of resurrection, and especially its
announcement in relation to Jesus, as political dynamite.[25]

The resurrection showed that Christ was and is the Son of God.
Wright:

[Believers] meant by this not simply that [Christ] was Israel's
Messiah, though that remained foundational; or simply that he
was the reality of which Caesar and all other tyrants were the
parodies, though that remained a vital implication. They meant
it in the sense that he was the personal embodiment and
revelation of the one true God [Wright had lower case].[26]

Thus, for their disparate reasons, both Jews and Romans hated
idea of the risen Jesus, he who, by his resurrection, was declared
to be the Son of God. Consequently, none of this can be
dismissed as a question of merely academic interest. The
penalties for not offering a pinch of incense at the Emperor's
shrine were severe.

Wright:

The whole point of passages like Romans 5:5-11; 8:3-4 and
Galatians 2:19-20; 4:4-7 is that what Jesus did in his public
career and supremely in his death was to be understood as the
work of 'God's Son'... *and that the resurrection declared that
this had been the case...* It declared that Jesus always was
'God's Son'... Paul is our earliest witness to the theology of the
first Christians, and already in his letters, within two or three
decades of Jesus' public [ministry],[27] we find it stated firmly
and clearly that the resurrection was the act of Israel's God, the
world's Creator, demonstrating that Jesus of Nazareth always
was his 'Son'... [Take] John's prologue (John 1:18)... Thomas:

---

[25] Wright pp729-730.
[26] Wright p731.
[27] Wright had 'career'.

the resurrection demonstrates that Jesus is 'my Lord and my God' [John 20:28].[28]

Wright summed it up:

> For a fuller picture, we would need to factor in the New Testament's talk of the Divine Spirit, the one who, the Christians believed, had been instrumental in God's raising of Jesus from the dead.[29]

> The early Christians... did not abandon their Jewish roots and adopt the language and thought-forms of paganism. They developed their theology by embracing one of the central Jewish beliefs of their day, the resurrection of the dead... This was what made them a messianic group within Judaism. This was what made them take on Caesar's world with the news that there was 'another king'. This was what made them not only speak of the one true God, but invoke him, pray to him, love him and serve him in terms of the Father and the [Lord],[30] of the God who sent the Son and now sends the Spirit of the Son, in terms of the only-begotten God who makes visible the otherwise invisible Creator of the world. This is why, when they spoke of the resurrection of Jesus, they spoke of the resurrection of the Son of God.[31]

> No wonder the Herods, the Caesars and the Sadducees of this world, ancient and modern, were and are eager to rule out all possibility of actual resurrection. They are, after all, staking a counter-claim on the real world. It is the real world that the tyrants and bullies (including intellectual and cultural tyrants and bullies) try to rule by force, only to discover that in order to do so they have to quash all rumours of resurrection, rumours that would imply that their greatest weapons – death and deconstruction – are not after all omnipotent.[32]

Many commentators interpret passages in Revelation as references to the battle between believers and the Romans over the State's demand for Emperor-worship. No wonder! Christ's

---

[28] Wright pp733-734, emphasis original.
[29] Wright p735.
[30] Wright had lower case.
[31] Wright p736.
[32] Wright p737.

resonant answer to the trick question – posed to try to make him blunder and so fall foul of the authorities – had set the agenda for believers:

> Render to Caesar the things that are Caesar's, and to God the things that are God's (Mark 12:13-17).

The early believers were taught to submit to the earthly powers where they could (Rom. 13:1-7; Tit. 3:1; 1 Pet. 2:13-17), but when it came to worship, when it came to preaching the gospel – especially with its emphasis upon Christ as King (or Prince – Acts 3:15; 5:31) – as we have seen, no compromise was allowed:

> Whether it is right in the sight of God to listen to you rather than to God, you must judge, for we cannot but speak of what we have seen and heard... We must obey God rather than men (Acts 4:19-20; 5:29).

Revelation 5 is a key passage. John 'saw in the right hand of him who was seated on the throne a scroll written within and on the back, sealed with seven seals' (Rev. 5:1). Only one person could break those seals and open that book: 'The Lion of the tribe of Judah, the Root of David, has conquered, so that he can open the scroll and its seven seals' (Rev. 5:5). John continued:

> I saw a Lamb standing, as though it had been slain, with seven horns and with seven eyes, which are the seven spirits of God sent out into all the earth. And he went and took the scroll from the right hand of him who was seated on the throne. And when he had taken the scroll, the four living creatures and the twenty-four elders fell down before the Lamb, each holding a harp, and golden bowls full of incense, which are the prayers of the saints. And they sang a new song, saying: 'Worthy are you to take the scroll and to open its seals, for you were slain, and by your blood you ransomed people for God from every tribe and language and people and nation, and you have made them a kingdom and priests to our God, and they shall reign on the earth' (Rev. 5:6-10).

The vision had not come to an end:

> Then I looked, and I heard around the throne and the living creatures and the elders the voice of many angels, numbering

myriads of myriads and thousands of thousands, saying with a loud voice: 'Worthy is the Lamb who was slain, to receive power and wealth and wisdom and might and honour and glory and blessing!'
And I heard every creature in heaven and on earth and under the earth and in the sea, and all that is in them, saying: 'To him who sits on the throne and to the Lamb be blessing and honour and glory and might forever and ever!'
And the four living creatures said: 'Amen!' and the elders fell down and worshipped (Rev. 5:11-14).

As for the seven seals, do not miss the repeated, triumphant chorus:

The Lamb opened one of the seven seals. [that is, the first]... he opened the second seal... he opened the third seal... the Lamb opened the seventh seal (Rev. 6:1,3,5,7,9,12; 8:1).

Jude, quoting Enoch, declared:

Behold, the Lord comes with ten thousands of his holy ones, to execute judgment on all and to convict all the ungodly of all their deeds of ungodliness that they have committed in such an ungodly way, and of all the harsh things that ungodly sinners have spoken against him (Jude 14-15).

He urged his fellow-believers:

But you, beloved, building yourselves up in your most holy faith and praying in the Holy Spirit, keep yourselves in the love of God, waiting for the mercy of our Lord Jesus Christ that leads to eternal life (Jude 20-21).

Returning to Revelation, do not fail to catch the tenor of John's opening of Christ's addresses to the seven churches in Asia, and how, right from the start, it set the tone for this triumphant book. John:

Grace to you and peace from him who is and who was and who is to come, and from the seven spirits who are before his throne, and from Jesus Christ the faithful witness, the firstborn of the dead, and the ruler of kings on earth.
To him who loves us and has freed us from our sins by his blood and made us a kingdom, priests to his God and Father, to him be glory and dominion forever and ever. Amen. Behold, he

is coming with the clouds, and every eye will see him, even those who pierced him, and all tribes of the earth will wail on account of him. Even so. Amen.
'I am the Alpha and the Omega," says the Lord God, "who is and who was and who is to come, the Almighty'.
I, John, your brother and partner in the tribulation and the kingdom and the patient endurance that are in Jesus, was on the island called Patmos on account of the word of God and the testimony of Jesus (Rev. 1:4-9).

As Christ was soon declaring:

Fear not, I am the first and the last, and the living one. I died, and behold I am alive forevermore, and I have the keys of death and Hades (Rev. 1:17-18).

What a claim!

As Christ said, introducing his letter to the *ekklēsia* at Smyrna:

The words of the first and the last, who died and came to life (Rev. 2:8).

And what a promise he gave to the *ekklēsia* at Thyatira:

Only hold fast what you have until I come. The one who conquers and who keeps my works until the end, to him I will give authority over the nations, and he will rule them with a rod of iron, as when earthen pots are broken in pieces, even as I myself have received authority from my Father. And I will give him the morning star (Rev. 2:25-28).

And to the lukewarm Laodiceans:

The one who conquers, I will grant him to sit with me on my throne, as I also conquered and sat down with my Father on his throne (Rev. 3:21).

And do not forget the repeated chorus: 'He who has an ear, let him hear what the Spirit says to the churches' (Rev. 2:7,11,17,29; 3:6,13,22).

While much of this was written to and for believers, it incidentally – but clearly – shows us the prominence of the resurrection in the way believers thought and what they preached when addressing unbelievers. There can be no doubt that such doctrine inevitably aroused the ire of the unconverted.

In short, confrontation was the hallmark of the way the early *ekklēsia* faced the surrounding cultures. And preaching Christ as King, shown by his resurrection, and all the implications of this doctrine, was at the very centre of this confrontation.

Use 2: Progressive Sanctification

Having looked at the major role which Christ's resurrection and kingship played in the way the first believers confronted the surrounding cultures by their rejection of, and separation from, paganism, and in their preaching of the gospel, I now turn to the part played by the resurrection and the kingdom in the progressive sanctification[1] of the first believers; as for the resurrection, I mean, of course, that of Christ himself, and of his people spiritually in him now and physically at his return.

So, how did the resurrection and the kingdom affect the early believer's progressive sanctification?

When writing to the Romans, having fully set out the doctrine of justification by faith alone, in Christ alone, on the basis of the grace of God alone (Rom. 1:16-17; 3:21 – 5:21),[2] Paul turned to the believer's progressive sanctification. In speaking of its necessity, its motive, its spring and its power, he made it clear that the resurrection of Christ is absolutely fundamental to the biblical doctrine and experience of the believer's progressive sanctification:

> What shall we say then? Are we to continue in sin that grace may abound? By no means! How can we who died to sin still live in it? Do you not know that all of us who have been [spiritually] baptised into Christ Jesus were [spiritually] baptised into his death?[3] We were buried therefore with him by [spiritual] baptism into death, in order that, just as Christ was raised from the dead by the glory of the Father, we too might walk in newness of life. For if [that is, since] we have been

---

[1] That is, the believer's practical and actual growth in Christ likeness (Rom. 8:29; Heb. 10:14; 12:14; 2 Pet. 3:18, and so on). I will not deal with the necessity of this progressive sanctification here, having done so elsewhere – see my *Fivefold*; *Liberty*.

[2] He drew on it again in Rom. 8:1.

[3] For my arguments justifying my claim that the baptism here is spiritual baptism (regeneration), not water baptism, see my *Baptist Sacramentalism*; *Infant*; *Hinge*.

united with him in a death like his, we shall certainly be united with him in a resurrection like his... Now if [that is, since] we have died with Christ, we believe that we will also live with him. We know that Christ, being raised from the dead, will never die again; death no longer has dominion over him. For the death he died he died to sin, once for all, but the life he lives he lives to God. So you also must consider yourselves dead to sin and alive to God in Christ Jesus Let not sin therefore reign in your mortal body, to make you obey its passions. Do not present your members to sin as instruments for unrighteousness, but present yourselves to God as those who have been brought from death to life, and your members to God as instruments for righteousness. For sin will have no dominion over you, since you are not under law but under grace... You... have died to the law through the body of Christ, so that you may belong to another, to him who has been raised from the dead, in order that we may bear fruit for God (Rom. 6:1-14; 7:4).

If [that is, since] the Spirit of him who raised Jesus from the dead dwells in you, he who raised Christ Jesus from the dead will also give life to your mortal bodies through his Spirit who dwells in you (Rom. 8:11).[4]

Clearly, Paul saw the resurrection as a major influence in progressive sanctification.

Similarly, when writing to the Corinthians about it, the apostle spoke of the resurrection and the kingdom:

Do you not know that the unrighteous will not inherit the kingdom of God? Do not be deceived: neither the sexually immoral, nor idolaters, nor adulterers, nor men who practice homosexuality, nor thieves, nor the greedy, nor drunkards, nor revilers, nor swindlers will inherit the kingdom of God. And such were some of you. But you were washed, you were sanctified, you were justified in the name of the Lord Jesus Christ and by the Spirit of our God (1 Cor. 6:9-11).

And:

---

[4] For more on the passage, in addition to my *Hinge* and *Infant*, see my *Christ*.

The love of Christ controls us, because we have concluded this: that one has died for all, therefore all have died; and he died for all, that those who live might no longer live for themselves but for him who for their sake died and was raised... Therefore, if anyone is in Christ, he is a new creation. The old has passed away; behold, the new has come (2 Cor. 5:4-17).

Addressing the Galatians, he had used the kingdom to press home his teaching on progressive sanctification:

Walk by the Spirit, and you will not gratify the desires of the flesh. For the desires of the flesh are against the Spirit, and the desires of the Spirit are against the flesh, for these are opposed to each other, to keep you from doing the things you want to do. But if you are led by the Spirit, you are not under the law. Now the works of the flesh are evident: sexual immorality, impurity, sensuality, idolatry, sorcery, enmity, strife, jealousy, fits of anger, rivalries, dissensions, divisions, envy, drunkenness, orgies, and things like these. I warn you, as I warned you before, that those who do such things will not inherit the kingdom of God. But the fruit of the Spirit is love, joy, peace, patience, kindness, goodness, faithfulness, gentleness, self-control; against such things there is no law. And those who belong to Christ Jesus have crucified the flesh with its passions and desires. If we live by the Spirit, let us also keep in step with the Spirit. Let us not become conceited, provoking one another, envying one another (Gal. 5:16-26).

Peter did the same:

The time that is past suffices for doing what the Gentiles want to do, living in sensuality, passions, drunkenness, orgies, drinking parties, and lawless idolatry. With respect to this they are surprised when you do not join them in the same flood of debauchery, and they malign you; but they will give account to him who is ready to judge the living and the dead (1 Pet. 4:3-5).

And Paul used the resurrection and exaltation of Christ in praying for the Ephesians that, among other things, they might:

...know what is the hope to which he has called you, what are the riches of his glorious inheritance in the saints, and what is the immeasurable greatness of his power toward us who believe, according to the working of his great might that he worked in Christ when he raised him from the dead and seated him at his right hand in the heavenly places (Eph. 1:18-20).

For what reason? Why all this talk of Christ's resurrection and kingdom, his rule, his governance? Surely, that believers might, by the felt experience of God's resurrection-power within them, live lives worthy of God:

> Therefore be imitators of God, as beloved children. And walk in love, as Christ loved us and gave himself up for us, a fragrant offering and sacrifice to God.
> But sexual immorality and all impurity or covetousness must not even be named among you, as is proper among saints. Let there be no filthiness nor foolish talk nor crude joking, which are out of place, but instead let there be thanksgiving. For you may be sure of this, that everyone who is sexually immoral or impure, or who is covetous (that is, an idolater), has no inheritance in the kingdom of Christ and God. Let no one deceive you with empty words, for because of these things the wrath of God comes upon the sons of disobedience. Therefore do not become partners with them; for at one time you were darkness, but now you are light in the Lord. Walk as children of light (for the fruit of light is found in all that is good and right and true), and try to discern what is pleasing to the Lord. Take no part in the unfruitful works of darkness, but instead expose them... (Eph. 5:1-11).

As Paul, when telling the Philippians about his conversion, explained, his desire – now converted[5] – was:

> ...that I may gain Christ and be found in him, not having a righteousness of my own that comes from the law, but that which comes through faith in Christ, the righteousness from God that depends on faith – that I may know him and the power of his resurrection, and may share his sufferings,

---

[5] Paul moves from justification (and positional sanctification) to progressive sanctification. If 'that I may gain... not having a righteousness of my own that comes from the law, but that which comes through faith in Christ, the righteousness from God that depends on faith' refers to progressive sanctification, what a direct contradiction of the position set out by Calvin and adopted by the Reformed – that the believer's progressive sanctification is by the law. See my *Christ*.

becoming like him in his death, that by any means possible I may attain the resurrection from the dead.
Not that I have already obtained this or am already perfect, but I press on to make it my own, because Christ Jesus has made me his own. Brothers, I do not consider that I have made it my own. But one thing I do: forgetting what lies behind and straining forward to what lies ahead, I press on toward the goal for the prize of the upward call of God in Christ Jesus. Let those of us who are mature think this way, and if in anything you think otherwise, God will reveal that also to you. Only let us hold true to what we have attained.
Brothers, join in imitating me, and keep your eyes on those who walk according to the example you have in us. For many, of whom I have often told you and now tell you even with tears, walk as enemies of the cross of Christ. Their end is destruction, their god is their belly, and they glory in their shame, with minds set on earthly things. But our citizenship is in heaven, and from it we await a Saviour, the Lord Jesus Christ, who will transform our lowly body to be like his glorious body, by the power that enables him even to subject all things to himself (Phil. 3:8-21).

Let me go back to the apostle's letter to the Ephesians; he declared:

And you were dead in the trespasses and sins in which you once walked, following the course of this world, following the prince of the power of the air, the spirit that is now at work in the sons of disobedience – among whom we all once lived in the passions of our flesh, carrying out the desires of the body and the mind, and were by nature children of wrath, like the rest of mankind. But God, being rich in mercy, because of the great love with which he loved us, even when we were dead in our trespasses, made us alive together with Christ – by grace you have been saved – and raised us up with him and seated us with him in the heavenly places in Christ Jesus, so that in the coming ages [that is, in the eternal kingdom of Christ] he might show the immeasurable riches of his grace in kindness toward us in Christ Jesus. For by grace you have been saved through faith. And this is not your own doing; it is the gift of God, not a result of works, so that no one may boast. For we are his workmanship, created in Christ Jesus for good works, which God prepared beforehand, that we should walk in them (Eph. 2:1-10).

And:

> I therefore, a prisoner for the Lord, urge you to walk in a manner worthy of the calling to which you have been called (Eph. 4:1).

Clearly, Paul was arguing for the believer's progressive sanctification on the basis of the resurrection – Christ's and the believer's – especially the believer's present spiritual resurrection in Christ, his felt sense within him of Christ in his resurrection power. And that was not all. The relationship of Christ to the believer – one of master/slave, husband/wife – is a vital strand in the apostle's argument. The kingship of Christ plays a major role in all this.

And although the apostle's argument in Ephesians 4:7-16 – concerning life in the *ekklēsia* – is not strictly about progressive sanctification, since one of the main aims of *ekklēsia* life is the believer's progressive sanctification – the Ephesian passage carries great weight in this regard. The incarnate, crucified and risen Christ gives gifts to his children for their edification, and the exercise of those gifts forms an integral part of *ekklēsia* life. Let us remind ourselves of what we have already seen:

> Let us consider how to stir up one another to love and good works, not neglecting to meet together, as is the habit of some, but encouraging one another, and all the more as you see the day [of judgment] drawing near (Heb. 10:24-25).

And that leads us straight to Ephesians 4:

> [Christ] gave the apostles, the prophets, the evangelists, the shepherds and teachers, to equip the saints for the work of ministry, for building up the body of Christ, until we all attain to the unity of the faith and of the knowledge of the Son of God, to mature manhood, to the measure of the stature of the fullness of Christ, so that we may no longer be children, tossed to and fro by the waves and carried about by every wind of doctrine, by human cunning, by craftiness in deceitful schemes. Rather, speaking the truth in love, we are to grow up in every way into him who is the head, into Christ, from whom the whole body, joined and held together by every joint with which

it is equipped, when each part is working properly, makes the body grow so that it builds itself up in love (Eph. 4:11-16).

Hence:

Now this I say and testify in the Lord, that you must no longer walk as the Gentiles do, in the futility of their minds. They are darkened in their understanding, alienated from the life of God because of the ignorance that is in them, due to their hardness of heart. They have become callous and have given themselves up to sensuality, greedy to practice every kind of impurity. But that is not the way you learned Christ! – assuming that you have heard about him and were taught in him, as the truth is in Jesus, to put off your old self, which belongs to your former manner of life and is corrupt through deceitful desires, and to be renewed in the spirit of your minds, and to put on the new self, created after the likeness of God in true righteousness and holiness... Sexual immorality and all impurity or covetousness must not even be named among you, as is proper among saints. Let there be no filthiness nor foolish talk nor crude joking, which are out of place, but instead let there be thanksgiving. For you may be sure of this, that everyone who is sexually immoral or impure, or who is covetous (that is, an idolater), has no inheritance in the kingdom of Christ and God (Eph. 4:17-24; 5:3-5).

Peter put *ekklēsia* life in light of the last day:

The end of all things is at hand; therefore be self-controlled and sober-minded for the sake of your prayers. Above all, keep loving one another earnestly, since love covers a multitude of sins. Show hospitality to one another without grumbling. As each has received a gift, use it to serve one another, as good stewards of God's varied grace: whoever speaks, as one who speaks oracles of God; whoever serves, as one who serves by the strength that God supplies – in order that in everything God may be glorified through Jesus Christ. To him belong glory and dominion forever and ever. Amen (1 Pet. 4:7-11).

What is more, let us remember what God said about spiritual Israelites in the days of the old covenant:

Then those who feared the LORD spoke with one another. The LORD paid attention and heard them, and a book of remembrance was written before him of those who feared the

LORD and esteemed his name. They shall be mine, says the LORD of hosts, in the day when I make up my treasured possession, and I will spare them as a man spares his son who serves him. Then once more you shall see the distinction between the righteous and the wicked, between one who serves God and one who does not serve him (Mal. 3:16-18).

Is this any less applicable to God's people – his special, precious chosen possession (1 Pet. 2:9-10) – in the days of the new covenant?

Consider Paul's letter to the believers at Colosse – do not miss the weight Paul gave to the resurrection and kingship of Christ:

> And so, from the day we heard [of your conversion], we have not ceased to pray for you, asking that you may be filled with the knowledge of his will in all spiritual wisdom and understanding, so as to walk in a manner worthy of the Lord, fully pleasing to him: bearing fruit in every good work and increasing in the knowledge of God; being strengthened with all power, according to his glorious might, for all endurance and patience with joy; giving thanks to the Father, who has qualified you to share in the inheritance of the saints in light. He has delivered us from the domain of darkness and transferred us to the kingdom of his beloved Son, in whom we have redemption, the forgiveness of sins (Col. 1:9-14).

And:

> [Christ] is the beginning, the firstborn from the dead, so that in everything he might be preeminent (Col. 1:18).

Do not miss the 'so that': Christ was raised in order that he might be preeminent in everything, he was raised in order to be chief and head of all things, he was raised in order to be declared to be the King, declared to be the Anointed, declared to be the Messiah, declared to be the Lord over all – especially over his people.

As Calvin put it in his *Commentary*:

> He is the beginning because he is the first-born from the dead; for in the resurrection there is a restoration of all things, and in this manner the commencement of the second and new creation, for the former had fallen to pieces in the ruin of the

first man. As, then, Christ in rising again had made a commencement of the kingdom of God, he is on good grounds called the beginning.

Having set out the glory of Christ, and his people's standing in him, on that basis, Paul went on to stir believers to progressive sanctification:

> Therefore, as you received Christ Jesus the Lord, so walk in him, rooted and built up in him and established in the faith, just as you were taught, abounding in thanksgiving. See to it that no one takes you captive by philosophy and empty deceit, according to human tradition, according to the elemental spirits of the world, and not according to Christ. For in him the whole fullness of deity dwells bodily, and you have been filled in him, who is the head of all rule and authority. In him also you were... raised with him through faith in the powerful working of God, who raised him from the dead. And you, who were dead in your trespasses and the uncircumcision of your flesh, God made alive together with him, having forgiven us all our trespasses, by cancelling the record of debt that stood against us with its legal demands (Col. 2:6-14).

And:

> [Since] then you have been raised with Christ, seek the things that are above, where Christ is, seated at the right hand of God. Set your minds on things that are above, not on things that are on earth. For you have died, and your life is hidden with Christ in God. When Christ who is your life appears, then you also will appear with him in glory. Put to death therefore what is earthly in you... seeing that you have put off the old self with its practices and have put on the new self, which is being renewed in knowledge after the image of its creator. Here there is not Greek and Jew, circumcised and uncircumcised, barbarian, Scythian, slave, free; but Christ is all, and in all (Col. 3:1-11).

In his earlier letter to the Thessalonians, the apostle had added an all-powerful motive and standard:

> We exhorted each one of you and encouraged you and charged you to walk in a manner worthy of God, who calls you into his own kingdom and glory (1 Thess. 2:12).

And, in his second letter:

> We ought always to give thanks to God for you, brothers, as is right, because your faith is growing abundantly, and the love of every one of you for one another is increasing. Therefore we ourselves boast about you in the churches of God for your steadfastness and faith in all your persecutions and in the afflictions that you are enduring. This is evidence of the righteous judgment of God, that you may be considered worthy of the kingdom of God, for which you are also suffering (2 Thess. 1:3-5).

The apostle spoke of the day of judgment:

> ...when [Christ] comes... to be glorified in his saints, and to be marvelled at among all who have believed... To this end we always pray for you, that our God may make you worthy of his calling and may fulfil every resolve for good and every work of faith by his power, so that the name of our Lord Jesus may be glorified in you, and you in him, according to the grace of our God and the Lord Jesus Christ (2 Thess. 1:10-12).

Again:

> We ought always to give thanks to God for you, brothers beloved by the Lord, because God chose you as the firstfruits to be saved, through sanctification by the Spirit and belief in the truth. To this he called you through our gospel, so that you may obtain the glory of our Lord Jesus Christ. So then, brothers, stand firm and hold to the traditions that you were taught by us, either by our spoken word or by our letter. Now may our Lord Jesus Christ himself, and God our Father, who loved us and gave us eternal comfort and good hope through grace, comfort your hearts and establish them in every good work and word (2 Thess. 2:13-17).

As he told Timothy:

> I charge you in the presence of God and of Christ Jesus, who is to judge the living and the dead, and by his appearing and his kingdom: preach the word; be ready in season and out of season; reprove, rebuke, and exhort, with complete patience and teaching (2 Tim. 4:1-2).

Peter wrote in the same vein to his readers:

[God's] divine power has granted to us all things that pertain to life and godliness, through the knowledge of him who called us to his own glory and excellence, by which he has granted to us his precious and very great promises, so that through them you may become partakers of the divine nature, having escaped from the corruption that is in the world because of sinful desire. For this very reason, make every effort to supplement your faith with virtue, and virtue with knowledge, and knowledge with self-control, and self-control with steadfastness, and steadfastness with godliness, and godliness with brotherly affection, and brotherly affection with love. For if these qualities are yours and are increasing, they keep you from being ineffective or unfruitful in the knowledge of our Lord Jesus Christ. For whoever lacks these qualities is so nearsighted that he is blind, having forgotten that he was cleansed from his former sins. Therefore, brothers, be all the more diligent to confirm your calling and election, for if you practice these qualities you will never fall. For in this way there will be richly provided for you an entrance into the eternal kingdom of our Lord and Saviour Jesus Christ (2 Pet. 1:3-11).

James spoke of 'the perfect law, the law of liberty', 'the royal law' (Jas. 1:25; 2:8), as that which governs believers to their progressive sanctification. Now however this law is defined – it must surely be 'the law of Christ' (1 Cor. 9:20-21; Gal. 6:2) – at the very least we may say it is the royal law in the sense of being the King's law.

And then we have this much debated passage;[6] whatever else it teaches, it clearly links Christ's resurrection with a believer's 'good conscience' – progressive sanctification, once again:

Baptism, which corresponds to this, now saves you, not as a removal of dirt from the body but as an appeal to God for a good conscience, through the resurrection of Jesus Christ, who has gone into heaven and is at the right hand of God, with angels, authorities, and powers having been subjected to him (1 Pet. 3:21-22).

And this must one of leading passages to make the point:

---

[6] For my view – that the baptism is spiritual baptism, regeneration – see my *Baptist Sacramentalism*.

The heavens and earth that now exist are stored up for fire, being kept until the day of judgment and destruction of the ungodly... The Lord is not slow to fulfil his promise as some count slowness, but is patient toward you, not wishing that any should perish, but that all should reach repentance. But the day of the Lord will come like a thief, and then the heavens will pass away with a roar, and the heavenly bodies will be burned up and dissolved, and the earth and the works that are done on it will be exposed. Since all these things are thus to be dissolved, what sort of people ought you to be in lives of holiness and godliness, waiting for and hastening the coming of the day of God, because of which the heavens will be set on fire and dissolved, and the heavenly bodies will melt as they burn! But according to his promise we are waiting for new heavens and a new earth in which righteousness dwells. Therefore, beloved, since you are waiting for these, be diligent to be found by him without spot or blemish, and at peace. And count the patience of our Lord as salvation... You therefore, beloved, knowing this beforehand, take care that you are not carried away with the error of lawless people and lose your own stability. But grow in the grace and knowledge of our Lord and Saviour Jesus Christ. To him be the glory both now and to the day of eternity. Amen (2 Pet. 3:7-18).

Moreover, since suffering is a part of progressive sanctification, believers must look on that in light of the coming kingdom:

I, John, your brother and partner in the tribulation and the kingdom and the patient endurance that are in Jesus... (Rev. 1:9).

John Bunyan certainly saw it that way. In his *The Pilgrim's Progress*, Evangelist, warning Christian and Faithful as they are about to face the testing and suffering in the town Vanity, urged them:

Let the kingdom be always before you, and believe steadfastly concerning things that are invisible... You must, through many tribulations, enter into the kingdom of heaven.

And the writer of Hebrews clearly set out the kingdom motive for progressive sanctification, which, as he said, is an absolute essential:

Strive for peace with everyone, and for the holiness without which no one will see the Lord... Let us be grateful for receiving a kingdom that cannot be shaken, and thus let us offer to God acceptable worship, with reverence and awe (Heb. 12:14,28).

This, too, is clinching:

Beloved, we are God's children now, and what we will be has not yet appeared; but we know that when he appears we shall be like him, because we shall see him as he is. And everyone who thus hopes in him purifies himself as he is pure (1 John 3:2-3).

Believers know that in the final day they will have to answer to Christ:

I tell you, on the day of judgment people will give account for every careless word they speak, for by your words you will be justified, and by your words you will be condemned (Matt. 12:36-37).[7]

While this must not be construed as teaching that a believer can be eternally condemned, nevertheless it does show that, in light of the return of Christ and the judgment, believers are conscious of the need for their daily walk with Christ to please and magnify their Redeemer:

And I saw the dead, great and small, standing before the throne, and books were opened. Then another book was opened, which is the book of life. And the dead were judged by what was written in the books, according to what they had done. And the sea gave up the dead who were in it, Death and Hades gave up the dead who were in them, and they were judged, each one of them, according to what they had done (Rev. 20:1-13).

Behold, I am coming soon, bringing my recompense with me, to repay everyone for what he has done (Rev. 22:12).

---

[7] As Calvin said in his *Commentary*: 'This is an argument from the less to the greater; for if every idle word is to be called in question, how would God spare the open blasphemies and sacrilegious insolence of those who bark against his glory?'

Hence:

> Brothers, be all the more diligent to confirm your calling and
> election, for if you practice these qualities you will never fall.
> For in this way there will be richly provided for you an
> entrance into the eternal kingdom of our Lord and Saviour
> Jesus Christ (2 Pet. 1:10-11).

> Therefore, beloved, since you are waiting for these, be diligent
> to be found by him without spot or blemish, and at peace... You
> therefore, beloved, knowing this beforehand, take care that you
> are not carried away with the error of lawless people and lose
> your own stability. But grow in the grace and knowledge of our
> Lord and Saviour Jesus Christ. To him be the glory both now
> and to the day of eternity. Amen (2 Pet. 3:14-18).[8]

It is beyond doubt: the first believers saw the resurrection of
Christ – and their own present spiritual resurrection in him –
coupled with his coming again in judgment as King – and their
present elevation to be spiritual priests and kings in him – as
mighty motives and motivators for their own progressive
sanctification.

Let Spurgeon, with a salutary warning, bring this chapter to a
close:

> Instead of acting like kings, many who claim to be the sons of
> God act as basely as if they were scullions in the kitchen of
> Mammon!
> What separation from the world, what exemplary holiness,
> what self-denial, what heavenly walking with God, ought to be
> seen in those who are chosen to be God's redeemed people, the
> representatives of God on earth!... O Lord, I know that in
> Christ Jesus, you have made me a king. Help me, then, to live a
> right royal life. Lay home to my conscience that question:
> 'What kind of person ought I to be?' And may I so answer it
> that I may live worthy of my high calling.[9]

---

[8] I quoted these passages again because of their powerful resonance in
what I am trying to say.
[9] C.H.Spurgeon: *Flowers from a Puritan's Garden.*

Use 3: The Believer's Hope

Having looked at how Christ's resurrection and his kingship influenced the first believers, both in their confrontation of sinners with the gospel and their own progressive sanctification, I turn, finally, to the part played in the 'blessed hope' of the first believers by Christ's resurrection and kingship.[1] When talking about what was the believer's hope, we are, of course, not talking about the believer's wishful thinking, but his certainty, his confident expectation, his assurance.

What is this hope, this confident anticipation which believers have in, through and despite all the changing circumstances of life, including persecution, and, in the ultimate, death? The believers' 'blessed hope' is the return of Christ as King and their resurrection leading to their entrance into his kingdom; as the apostle so clearly stated, it is:

> ...the appearing of the glory of our great God and Saviour Jesus Christ (Tit. 2:13).

The Believer's Hope in Persecution

I turn, first of all, to the believer's comfort in persecution (which surely covers the believer's comfort in all kinds of affliction). Scripture is clear:

> Blessed are those who are persecuted for righteousness' sake, for theirs is the kingdom of heaven. Blessed are you when others revile you and persecute you and utter all kinds of evil against you falsely on my account. Rejoice and be glad, for your reward is great in heaven (Matt. 5:10-12).

> Blessed is the man who remains steadfast under trial, for when he has stood the test he will receive the crown of life, which God has promised to those who love him (Jas. 1:12).

---

[1] For a discourse I preached when writing this present work, see my 'Looking Forward – To What?' on my sermonaudio.com page and You Tube.

I know your tribulation and your poverty (but you are rich) and the slander of those who say that they are Jews and are not, but are a synagogue of Satan. Do not fear what you are about to suffer. Behold, the devil is about to throw some of you into prison, that you may be tested, and for ten days you will have tribulation. Be faithful unto death, and I will give you the crown of life. He who has an ear, let him hear what the Spirit says to the churches. The one who conquers will not be hurt by the second death (Rev. 2:9-11).

What is the believer's comfort in trial? The reward, the crown, the recognition that is already prepared for him in heaven. But we need to pause at this point. We must be clear about this mention of 'in heaven'. True, believers' rewards are already reserved for them in heaven (Matt. 5:12; 6:19-23; 19:21; Luke 12:33-34; 18:22; 1 Pet. 1:4), but when do they receive them? In the intermediate state? No! At the appearance of Christ the King, and their resurrection to the last judgment; that is the final day, the reckoning day:

For the Son of Man is going to come with his angels in the glory of his Father, and then he will repay each person according to what he has done (Matt. 16:27).

[God] commands all people everywhere to repent, because he has fixed a day on which he will judge the world in righteousness by a man whom he has appointed; and of this he has given assurance to all by raising him from the dead (Acts 17:30-31).

Each one's work will become manifest, for the Day will disclose it, because it will be revealed by fire, and the fire will test what sort of work each one has done. If the work that anyone has built on the foundation survives, he will receive a reward. If anyone's work is burned up, he will suffer loss, though he himself will be saved, but only as through fire (1 Cor. 3:13-15).

For we must all appear before the judgment seat of Christ, so that each one may receive what is due for what he has done in the body, whether good or evil (2 Cor. 5:10).

For what is our hope or joy or crown of boasting before our Lord Jesus at his coming? Is it not you? (1 Thess. 2:19).

I pray God your whole spirit and soul and body be preserved blameless unto the coming of our Lord Jesus Christ (1 Thess. 5:23).

Your steadfastness and faith in all your persecutions and in the afflictions that you are enduring... is evidence of the righteous judgment of God, that you may be considered worthy of the kingdom of God, for which you are also suffering – since indeed God considers it just to repay with affliction those who afflict you, and to grant relief to you who are afflicted as well as to us, when the Lord Jesus is revealed from heaven with his mighty angels in flaming fire, inflicting vengeance on those who do not know God and on those who do not obey the gospel of our Lord Jesus... Now concerning the coming of our Lord Jesus Christ and our being gathered together to him... (2 Thess. 1:4-8; 2:1).

Keep the commandment unstained and free from reproach until the appearing of our Lord Jesus Christ, which he will display at the proper time – he who is the blessed and only Sovereign, the King of kings and Lord of Lords (1 Tim. 6:14-15).

Henceforth there is laid up for me the crown of righteousness, which the Lord, the righteous judge, will award to me on that Day, and not only to me but also to all who have loved his appearing (2 Tim. 4:8).

Be patient, therefore, brothers, until the coming of the Lord. See how the farmer waits for the precious fruit of the earth, being patient about it, until it receives the early and the late rains. You also, be patient. Establish your hearts, for the coming of the Lord is at hand. Do not grumble against one another, brothers, so that you may not be judged; behold, the Judge is standing at the door (Jas. 5:7-9).

Keep your conduct among the Gentiles honourable, so that when they speak against you as evildoers, they may see your good deeds and glorify God on the day of visitation (1 Pet. 2:12).

And when the chief Shepherd appears, you will receive the unfading crown of glory (1 Pet. 5:4).

I am coming soon. Hold fast what you have, so that no one may seize your crown (Rev. 3:11).

And I saw the dead, great and small, standing before the throne, and books were opened. Then another book was opened, which is the book of life. And the dead were judged by what was written in the books, according to what they had done. And the sea gave up the dead who were in it, Death and Hades gave up the dead who were in them, and they were judged, each one of them, according to what they had done (Rev. 20:1-13).

Behold, I am coming soon, bringing my recompense with me, to repay everyone for what he has done (Rev. 22:12).

This is not the end of the scriptures which show that believers' hope in face of trial and persecution lies in their resurrection at the return of Christ, and their entrance into his eternal kingdom, the eternal age:

Truly, I say to you, there is no one who has left house or brothers or sisters or mother or father or children or lands, for my sake and for the gospel, who will not receive a hundredfold now in this time, houses and brothers and sisters and mothers and children and lands, with persecutions, and in the age to come eternal life (Mark 10:29-30).

Beloved, do not be surprised at the fiery trial when it comes upon you to test you, as though something strange were happening to you. But rejoice insofar as you share Christ's sufferings, that you may also rejoice and be glad when his glory is revealed. If you are insulted for the name of Christ, you are blessed, because the Spirit of glory and of God rests upon you (1 Pet. 4:12-14).

Because you have kept my word about patient endurance, I will keep you from the hour of trial that is coming on the whole world, to try those who dwell on the earth. I am coming soon. Hold fast what you have, so that no one may seize your crown. The one who conquers, I will make him a pillar in the temple of my God. Never shall he go out of it, and I will write on him the name of my God, and the name of the city of my God, the new Jerusalem, which comes down from my God out of heaven, and my own new name. He who has an ear, let him hear what the Spirit says to the churches (Rev. 3:10-13).

Clearly, the 'blessed hope' which encouraged the first believers in face of inevitable affliction and trial was Christ's return, their resurrection and subsequent entrance into the Saviour's kingdom.

The Believer's Hope in Death

Now for the ultimate issue – death. What is the 'blessed hope', the confident anticipation which believers have in facing death, their final enemy (1 Cor. 15:26)? Judging by the way many funeral hymns and sermons seem to major on it, in facing bereavement and death most believers find comfort in the 'blessed hope' of a glorious intermediate state; that is to say, the thought that the believer, at death, immediately enters heaven to enjoy the full experience of eternal glory with Christ, linked with reunion with previously-deceased fellow-believers, especially loved-relations.[2] This, for many believers, is what constitutes their comfort and consolation. Indeed, graveyards are packed with headstones carved with such an assurance.

But, while Scripture does teach that a believer is always 'with Christ', in life, through death, and after death (Rom. 14:9; Heb. 13:5-6), the believer's 'blessed hope' – according to Scripture – is not the intermediate state, but Christ's coming again, with the believer's resurrection into Christ's kingdom, all depending on Christ's own resurrection.[3]

---

[2] These verses need to be pondered: 'No one has ascended into heaven except he who descended from heaven, the Son of Man' (John 3:13). 'David... both died and was buried, and his tomb is with us to this day... David did not ascend into the heavens' (Acts 2:29,34). 'Whom have I in heaven but you?' (Ps. 73:25).

[3] One of the grievous aspects of the post-millennialism I referred to in the Introduction (see also Appendix 1) is that those who hold that view are looking forward to the fulfilment of a hope before Christ's return. In their view, the kingdom will come in indescribable joy *before* Christ returns: his coming will, in effect, interrupt that joy in order to reinstate it! This dream is based, not on any plain scripture which addresses believers, but on a theological or prophetical scheme. The title of the leading contemporary Reformed book advocating such a kingdom, and which has powerfully affected writers like Sarah James, for instance – *The Puritan Hope* by Iain Murray – gives the game away. Such a kingdom may have been the hope of many puritans, but that cannot be

Again, we must never forget or ignore the big picture. Ever since Adam's fall, creation – including and especially man – has been cursed, cursed by God as a result of sin. First, God addressed the serpent:

> Because you have done this, cursed are you above all livestock and above all beasts of the field; on your belly you shall go, and dust you shall eat all the days of your life. I will put enmity between you and the woman, and between your offspring and her offspring; he shall bruise your head, and you shall bruise his heel.

Then the woman:

> I will surely multiply your pain in childbearing; in pain you shall bring forth children. Your desire shall be contrary to your husband, but he shall rule over you.

And finally, Adam:

> Because you have listened to the voice of your wife and have eaten of the tree of which I commanded you: 'You shall not eat of it', cursed is the ground because of you; in pain you shall eat of it all the days of your life; thorns and thistles it shall bring forth for you; and you shall eat the plants of the field. By the sweat of your face you shall eat bread, till you return to the ground, for out of it you were taken; for you are dust, and to dust you shall return' (Gen. 3:14-19).

Indeed, disorder, confusion and division became the order of the day, following God's curse on the world at Babel (Gen. 11:1-9).

But God always intended to renew the fallen and ruined creation:

> I consider that the sufferings of this present time are not worth comparing with the glory that is to be revealed to [or in or upon] us. For the creation waits with eager longing for the revealing of the sons of God. For the creation was subjected to

---

decisive: Does Scripture refer to such a kingdom when it speaks of the believer's 'blessed hope'? Which apostle wrote of it? For those who might suggest Paul in Rom. 9–11, see my *Romans 11*. As everybody knows, the puritans had to come to terms with defeat, and the dashing of so many of their hopes. See my *Battle*.

futility, not willingly, but because of him who subjected it, in hope that the creation itself will be set free from its bondage to corruption and obtain the freedom of the glory of the children of God. For we know that the whole creation has been groaning together in the pains of childbirth until now. And not only the creation, but we ourselves, who have the firstfruits of the Spirit, groan inwardly as we wait eagerly for adoption as sons, the redemption of our bodies. For in this hope we were saved. Now hope that is seen is not hope. For who hopes for what he sees? But if we hope for what we do not see, we wait for it with patience (Rom. 8:18-25).

Paul, writing to the Ephesians, spoke of it:

...the mystery of [God's] will, according to his purpose, which he set forth in Christ as a plan for the fullness of time, to unite all things in him, things in heaven and things on earth (Eph. 1:9-10).

Peter, too:

The heavens and earth that now exist are stored up for fire, being kept until the day of judgment and destruction of the ungodly... The day of the Lord will come like a thief, and then the heavens will pass away with a roar, and the heavenly bodies will be burned up and dissolved, and the earth and the works that are done on it will be exposed [destroyed]... The heavens will be set on fire and dissolved, and the heavenly bodies will melt as they burn! But according to his promise we are waiting for new heavens and a new earth in which righteousness dwells (2 Pet. 3:7,10,12-13).

And John could declare:

I saw a new heaven and a new earth, for the first heaven and the first earth had passed away, and the sea was no more... God... will wipe away every tear from their eyes, and death shall be no more, neither shall there be mourning, nor crying, nor pain anymore, for the former things have passed away (Rev. 21:1-4).[4]

---

[4] 'The wolf shall dwell with the lamb, and the leopard shall lie down with the young goat, and the calf and the lion and the fattened calf together; and a little child shall lead them. The cow and the bear shall graze; their young shall lie down together; and the lion shall eat straw

While not for a moment suggesting that the following verses speak of universal redemption, even so they do indicate Christ's redemptive work will lead to a gloriously positive end for all creation. Take, for instance, Peter's assertion concerning:

...Jesus, whom heaven must receive until the time for restoring all the things about which God spoke by the mouth of his holy prophets long ago (Acts 3:20-21).

And Paul could speak of the time:

...when all things are [that is, will be] subjected to him [that is, Christ]... (1 Cor. 15:28).

...the power that enables him [that is, the Lord Jesus Christ] even to subject all things to himself (Phil. 3:21).

He is the image of the invisible God, the firstborn of all creation. For by him all things were created, in heaven and on earth, visible and invisible, whether thrones or dominions or rulers or authorities – all things were created through him and for him. And he is before all things, and in him all things hold together. And he is the head of the body, the church. He is the beginning, the firstborn from the dead, so that in everything he might be preeminent. For in him all the fullness of God was pleased to dwell, and through him to reconcile to himself all things, whether on earth or in heaven, making peace by the blood of his cross (Col. 1:15-20).

And believers are the glorious forerunners of this new creation – as James reminded his readers:

Of his own will [the Father] brought us forth by the word of truth, that we should be a kind of firstfruits of his creatures (Jas. 1:18).

---

like the ox. The nursing child shall play over the hole of the cobra, and the weaned child shall put his hand on the adder's den. They shall not hurt or destroy in all my holy mountain; for the earth shall be full of the knowledge of the LORD as the waters cover the sea' (Isa. 11:6-9). "'The wolf and the lamb shall graze together; the lion shall eat straw like the ox, and dust shall be the serpent's food. They shall not hurt or destroy in all my holy mountain", says the LORD' (Isa. 65:25).

This is the big picture. And Scripture places the believer's hope securely within this overall plan of God. Let me prove it.

I start with what I have already called[5] the principal passage:

> Now I would remind you, brothers, of the gospel I preached to you, which you received, in which you stand, and by which you are being saved, if you hold fast to the word I preached to you – unless you believed in vain. For I delivered to you as of first importance what I also received: that Christ died for our sins in accordance with the Scriptures, that he was buried, that he was raised on the third day in accordance with the Scriptures... So we preach and so you believed.
>
> Now if Christ is proclaimed as raised from the dead, how can some of you say that there is no resurrection of the dead? But if there is no resurrection of the dead, then not even Christ has been raised. And if Christ has not been raised, then our preaching is in vain and your faith is in vain. We are even found to be misrepresenting God, because we testified about God that he raised Christ, whom he did not raise if it is true that the dead are not raised. For if the dead are not raised, not even Christ has been raised. And if Christ has not been raised, your faith is futile and you are still in your sins. Then those also who have fallen asleep in Christ have perished. If in Christ we have hope in this life only, we are of all people most to be pitied.
>
> But in fact Christ has been raised from the dead, the firstfruits of those who have fallen asleep. For as by a man came death, by a man has come also the resurrection of the dead. For as in Adam all die, so also in Christ shall all be made alive. But each in his own order: Christ the firstfruits, then at his coming those who belong to Christ. Then comes the end, when he delivers the kingdom to God the Father after destroying every rule and every authority and power. For he must reign until he has put all his enemies under his feet. The last enemy to be destroyed is death...
>
> Otherwise, what do people mean by being baptised on behalf of the dead? If the dead are not raised at all, why are people baptised on their behalf? Why are we in danger every hour? I protest, brothers, by my pride in you, which I have in Christ Jesus our Lord, I die every day! What do I gain if, humanly

---

[5] I quote this passage again to make sure the point is driven home.

speaking, I fought with beasts at Ephesus? If the dead are not raised: 'Let us eat and drink, for tomorrow we die'...

...the resurrection of the dead... What is sown is perishable; what is raised is imperishable. It is sown in dishonour; it is raised in glory. It is sown in weakness; it is raised in power. It is sown a natural body; it is raised a spiritual body. If there is a natural body, there is also a spiritual body. Thus it is written: 'The first man Adam became a living being', the last Adam became a life-giving spirit. But it is not the spiritual that is first but the natural, and then the spiritual. The first man was from the earth, a man of dust; the second man is from heaven. As was the man of dust, so also are those who are of the dust, and as is the man of heaven, so also are those who are of heaven. Just as we have borne the image of the man of dust, we shall also bear the image of the man of heaven.

I tell you this, brothers: flesh and blood cannot inherit the kingdom of God, nor does the perishable inherit the imperishable. Behold! I tell you a mystery. We shall not all sleep, but we shall all be changed, in a moment, in the twinkling of an eye, at the last trumpet. For the trumpet will sound, and the dead will be raised imperishable, and we shall be changed. For this perishable body must put on the imperishable, and this mortal body must put on immortality. When the perishable puts on the imperishable, and the mortal puts on immortality, then shall come to pass the saying that is written: 'Death is swallowed up in victory. O death, where is your victory? O death, where is your sting?'

The sting of death is sin, and the power of sin is the law. But thanks be to God, who gives us the victory through our Lord Jesus Christ.

Therefore, my beloved brothers, be steadfast, immovable, always abounding in the work of the Lord, knowing that in the Lord your labour is not in vain (1 Cor. 15:1-58).

What is the believer's hope, the believer's consolation at the graveside of a fellow-believer, and his assurance in facing his own death? Is it the intermediate state? It is not! It is the resurrection of Christ and hence the believer's own resurrection with all the saints at the last day! Indeed, as the extract proves, the very act of burial confidently proclaims – and proclaims in the utmost clarity – the sowing of a seed, knowing that it will perish in the ground, but, in due time, will lead to the arising of a glorious new life. Christ promulgated this truth just before his own death:

> The hour has come for the Son of Man to be glorified. Truly, truly, I say to you, unless a grain of wheat falls into the earth and dies, it remains alone; but if it dies, it bears much fruit (John 12:23-24).[6]

This expectation is encapsulated in Christ's ringing assertion at the grave of Lazarus: 'He shall rise again' (John 11:23). And it is this that should give every believer comfort at the death of a fellow–believer – and when they come to their own experience of grappling with the last dread enemy (1 Cor. 15:26,54-55; Heb. 2:14-15).

But even that does not plumb the depths of Christ's words. As Charles Ellicott commented:

> [Martha] has spoken of the resurrection as a truth which she believes, and as an event in the far-off future, so remote from the present life indeed, as to be powerless to comfort her now ['I know that he will rise again in the resurrection on the last day' (John 11:24)]. The two first words of [Christ's] answer, expressed in the fullness of emphasis, teach her that the resurrection is to be thought of as his person, and that it is to be thought of as actually present. 'I' – his words mean – 'and none beside me, am the resurrection. I am the resurrection – a present life, and not simply a life in the remoteness of the last day'. In the same sense in which he has declared himself to be the water of life and the bread of life, supplying in himself every need of spiritual thirst and spiritual hunger, he declares himself to be the resurrection, revealing in his own person all that men had ever thought and hoped of a future life, being himself the power which shall raise them at the last day, and

---

[6] This principle is one of the main reasons why I oppose cremation; at a stroke, it grievously obliterates the most important spiritual lesson to be learned from the burial of a cadaver in the earth: sowing a seed to produce new life. Cremation, it seems to me, marks the atheist's desire, at all costs, to get rid of any thought of God wherever he can: destroy the body; whatever the Bible promises, that body cannot rise! But, of course, it will!

could therefore raise them now. This is because he is also 'the life'.

In other words, the resurrection is not simply an event at the end of time; it is not a mantra or slogan to be repeated as some sort of catechism. Martha, it seems, had got no further than that. Resurrection at Christ's appearing, of course, marks the end of time, but the resurrection, in a spiritual sense, is here and now for those in Christ. Moreover, Christ does not say: 'I will raise...', but: 'I – I myself – am the resurrection'. And all those who are in the new covenant are in union with Christ by faith, and raised with him spiritually, even now. This, it goes without saying, does not detract in the slightest from the believer's physical resurrection at the last day. Rather, it provides yet another link between the believer's 'blessed hope' and his present life in Christ: he is raised to newness of life in the Spirit, even now.

This, then, is the believer's hope, his 'blessed hope' – 'the appearing of the glory of our great God and Saviour Jesus Christ' (Tit. 2:13); in other words, the believer's 'blessed hope' is the thought of his glorious resurrection at the coming of Christ. It is not his happiness in anticipating the intermediate state: that is, his bliss after death and before the resurrection.

Consider another passage, a passage of huge significance in this matter. If ever there was a time and place for an apostle to reassure believers, anxious about their believing dead, by telling them about the present blessed state of those who had died trusting Christ, it must have been when Paul was writing to the saints at Thessalonica, dealing with this very issue:

> We do not want you to be uninformed, brothers, about those who are asleep [that is, those believers who have died], that you may not grieve as others do who have no hope. For since we believe that Jesus died and rose again, even so, through Jesus, God will bring with him those who have fallen asleep. For this we declare to you by a word from the Lord, that we who are alive, who are left until the coming of the Lord, will not precede those who have fallen asleep. For the Lord himself will descend from heaven with a cry of command, with the

voice of an archangel, and with the sound of the trumpet of God. And the dead in Christ will rise first. Then we who are alive, who are left, will be caught up together with them in the clouds to meet the Lord in the air, and so we will always be with the Lord. Therefore encourage one another with these words (1 Thess. 4:13-18).

Paul's silence about the intermediate state, when writing to these anxious believers in Thessalonica, knocks Sherlock Holmes' 'curious incident' on Dartmoor into a cocked hat.[7]

Why! the Thessalonians' concern would not arise today; I have never met a believer who was worried that some believing loved-one who had died might be overlooked when Christ returns. After all, the vast majority of believers are convinced that the loved-one in question is already enjoying glory with Christ even now – so how could he or she be overlooked? But the Thessalonians *were* in agony over this very point. Why?

But let us not leave it in the negative. Do not miss the positive confidence in these words:

> For this we declare to you by a word from the Lord, that we who are alive, who are left until the coming of the Lord, will not precede those who have fallen asleep. For the Lord himself will descend from heaven with a cry of command, with the voice of an archangel, and with the sound of the trumpet of God. And the dead in Christ will rise first. Then we who are alive, who are left, will be caught up together with them in the clouds to meet the Lord in the air, and so we will always be with the Lord. Therefore encourage one another with these words

Indeed, there is no shortage of scriptural testimony to show that the believer's hope is the return of Christ, the resurrection, and the transformation of the believer's mortal body into an immortal body at the last day, leading to eternal bliss in Christ's kingdom. As the writer to the Hebrews said: 'Here we have no lasting city, but we seek the city that is to come' (Heb. 11:14).

---

[7] See Conan Doyle's *The Adventure of Silver Blaze*.

This, of course, is just as it was with Abraham and his fellow-believers spoken of in Hebrews 11:

> By faith Abraham obeyed when he was called to go out to a place that he was to receive as an inheritance. And he went out, not knowing where he was going. By faith he went to live in the land of promise, as in a foreign land, living in tents with Isaac and Jacob, heirs with him of the same promise. For he was looking forward to the city that has foundations, whose designer and builder is God... These all died in faith, not having received the things promised, but having seen them and greeted them from afar, and having acknowledged that they were strangers and exiles on the earth. For people who speak thus make it clear that they are seeking a homeland. If they had been thinking of that land from which they had gone out, they would have had opportunity to return. But as it is, they desire a better country, that is, a heavenly one. Therefore God is not ashamed to be called their God, for he has prepared for them a city (Heb. 11:8-16).

And when will that city come? At the return of Christ!

What is it, specifically, about the believer's resurrection that makes it the time of his 'blessed hope'? Surely, it must be that it marks his entrance into Christ's kingdom in all its fullness. True, right from his conversion – his regeneration leading to saving repentance towards God and trust in Christ – the child of God has been in the kingdom. Indeed, right from eternity, in God's decree, it has been so. But it is only with his resurrection at Christ's return that the believer will enjoy to the full the realities and glories of that everlasting kingdom. It is only then that the believer will receive his resurrected body (John 5:25,28; 11:24; 1 Cor. 15:22-23; Phil. 3:20-21), enabling him to enjoy the new heavens and the new earth.[8]

---

[8] An objection: Doesn't 2 Cor. 5:1-10 teach that at death the believer is clothed with his new body? I think not. As Paul states: 'We know that while we are at home in the body we are away from the Lord, for we walk by faith, not by sight. Yes, we are of good courage, and we would rather be away from the body and at home with the Lord' (2 Cor. 5:6-8). To be with Christ (in the intermediate state) is to be 'absent from the body' – which is decomposing in the earth. Moreover, we know

So much for the believer's 'blessed hope'.

* * *

I do not wish to give the impression that these things exist in watertight compartments. The believer's progressive sanctification, his 'blessed hope' and his life in the *ekklēsia* are all bound together in Christ, in his death, resurrection and return.

In dealing with the spiritual union of Christ and his people, Emil Brunner set out the unbreakable link between Christ's death and his resurrection:

---

that the believer receives his resurrected body at the resurrection (1 Cor. 15:35-57). Ellicott: 'The answer to that question [that is, the question I am dealing with] is found in the manifest fact that the intermediate state occupied but a subordinate position in... Paul's thoughts... He did not speculate accordingly about that [intermediate] state, but was content to rest in the belief that when absent from the body he would, in some more immediate sense, be present with the Lord. But the longing of his soul was... that the Lord might come quickly – that he might put on the new and glorious body'. Gill: '...which is meant not the glorified body in the resurrection morn; for though the bodies of the saints will be glorious, incorruptible, powerful, and spiritual, they are not said to be celestial, nor will they be from heaven, but be raised out of the earth'. Calvin, while he was not absolutely certain, showed where he planted his feet: 'The body, such as we now have it, [Paul] calls a house of tabernacle For as tabernacles are constructed for a temporary purpose of slight materials, and without any firm foundation, and then shortly afterwards are thrown down, or fall of their own accord, so the mortal body is given to men as a frail hut, to be inhabited by them for a few days... 2 Pet. 1:13; Job 4:19... a house of clay. [The apostle] places in contrast with this a building of perpetual duration. It is not certain whether he means by this term a state of blessed immortality, which awaits believers after death, or the incorruptible and glorious body, such as it will be after the resurrection. In whichever of these senses it is taken, it will not be unsuitable; though I prefer to understand it as meaning that the blessed condition of the soul after death is the commencement of this building, and the glory of the final resurrection is the consummation of it'.

The fellowship of Jesus discloses a paradoxical unity of terms which elsewhere are incompatible. It is a spiritual[9] unity of visible earthly persons with an unseen, heavenly, and yet present person, their Head... the eternal ever-present Christ... This invisible Christ, the Lord, is in fact no other than he whom the... apostles... had known in the flesh as the rabbi, Jesus of Nazareth, with whom they had eaten and walked in bodily fellowship, who had been amongst them in his physical presence on the last evening of his life and who on the day following had been crucified. And his death upon the cross was a very real and tangible fact of history... It was not something which now lived forever behind them as though it had been revoked by the subsequent fact of the resurrection: much rather, the fact of his having been crucified was the saving fact itself upon which all their faith was founded. Only in the unity of the cross and the resurrection was the life of faith possible as a being crucified with Christ, and at the same time a sharing in his triumphant life.

But, as the first believers found, it was only after their conversion that they began to grasp this amazing fact:

Not until they had risen with him in their hearts did they apprehend within themselves his... spiritual presence[10]... which lives entirely in the life of a historical, never-to-be-repeated occurrence and is actually identical with this occurrence... (Gal. 2:20).

Brunner moved from the past and present to the future:

This community [that is, the *ekklēsia*] knows itself to be not only bound up with the saving history of the past, rooted in it and living in it, but also essentially looking forward to a salvation which is yet to come. The *ekklēsia* as the fellowship of the Messiah is itself messianic: its existence can be properly described only by using the categories of eschatology, or expectation of a transcendent consummation. This consummation has dawned with Jesus; in his incarnate life it has already begun... The kingdom of God has come (Matt. 12:28; Luke 11:20); the rule of God for which all are looking is

---

[9] Original 'mystical'. This applies throughout these extracts from Brunner.

[10] Original 'so-called mystical presence'.

already among you, for he the transcendent eternal Messiah is already in their midst (Luke 17:21; Matt. 18:20). But as yet it was a concealed presence. Only with the resurrection did the veil begin to be withdrawn. His presence among them as the risen one is a transcendent happening, 'realised eschatology'...
The new age has now dawned. And yet, at the same time, it remains unfulfilled; in its plenitude it has still to be awaited. This expectation of the future consummation as distinguished from the salvation which has already been realised cannot be dismissed as a more or less ancillary element in the life of the Christian community; it is the very breath of its life...
To live in this hope, in this tense expectation of the transcendent goal, and from that standpoint to view this here-and-now as a preliminary – that is precisely the fundamental character of the community's life. They 'have, as though they had not' (1 Cor. 7:29f). And further: precisely this forward-looking attitude is identical with what they term the gift of the Holy Ghost. For he, the Holy Ghost, is the very life of the new age. *He* is the 'realised eschatology'. For they qualify the gift of the Holy Spirit as the first-fruits, the earnest, the Pledge of the future. To be in the Spirit and to live in this expectation are one and the same thing. Therefore they know that their material life on earth, in this sinful body, subjected to the sinful ordinances of this world and chained to the body of this death, is a not-yet-having. They are therefore pilgrims on earth; they know that this earthly life is but a provisional dispensation which will not be transformed into the finality of eternal heavenly life until the Lord comes again in glory.
They walk as yet 'by faith, not by sight' (2 Cor. 5:7)...
Everywhere it is implied that the new life is a life on the threshold, and everywhere it is just the possession of the Holy Spirit which determines and characterises that life on the threshold.
The spiritual is the eschatological and the eschatological is spiritual.

Brunner was clear as to the connection between the rise of the institution of the Church (that is, Christendom) and the decline of the believers' expectation of Christ's return and the kingdom:

The tendency to exalt the [ecclesiastical] office as such could not arise as long as men's hearts and hopes were set upon the future, and in consequence the present dispensation regarded as provisional merely. The emergence of ecclesiastical rule and jurisdiction is coincident with the loss or weakening of the community's messianic consciousness. Both the pneumatic and the messianic factors work in the same direction. As long as they are sufficiently alive, they prevent and render superfluous all institutional consolidation. The community which waits in hope for the return of the Lord, and which lives by faith and love in the possession of his Spirit, cannot be an institution, a church.[11]

---

[11] Emil Brunner: *The Misunderstanding of the Church*, Lutterworth Press, London, 1952, pp55-59, emphasis original..

Application

In applying what we have seen, I will employ the same three headings used in the previous chapters – confrontation, consecration and comfort. In a sense, I have already started to make application by remarks along the way; even more fundamentally, by my chosen title: I am convinced that we, as modern evangelicals, seriously undervalue how Christ's resurrection and kingdom ought to dominate our evangelism, our efforts for personal holiness, and our sense of consolation. In this brief chapter, I want to do something towards redressing this.

Confrontation

The first believers knew that they were surrounded by, and confronted by, hostile cultures – whether Jewish, Graeco-Roman or downright heathen – and they knew contemporary society was hostile to them and the gospel because it was hostile to Christ. The early believers could have compromised – compromised themselves, the gospel and the *ekklēsia* – with those cultures, and survived. Indeed, they could have gone further: they could not only have adapted the gospel to the world, they could have adopted some of the leading principles of those cultures in order to make the gospel acceptable to fallen men and women, and thus become part of the acceptable establishment, even leaders of it. They did not; the first believers did none of it.[1] Rather, as we have seen, they sought

---

[1] Of course, in order to communicate with their hearers they went as far as could without compromising the gospel. They made full use of the synagogue-opportunity open to them as Jews (Acts 9:20; 13:5,14-15; 14:1; 17:1,10.17; 18:4-26); they would have private conversation with Jewish leaders (Acts 28:17-29), and preach to any Jews who were willing to come and hear (Acts 28:30-31). As for Gentiles, see Acts 10 on. Paul set out his thinking: 'Though I am free from all, I have made myself a servant to all, that I might win more of them. To the Jews I became as a Jew, in order to win Jews. To those under the law I

143

God's help and power to be bold – fearless, uncompromising – in their preaching and living, pulling no punches in what they said when addressing the surrounding cultures. And one word encapsulates it: 'confrontation'. By preaching the crucified and risen Christ, the Messiah, the King and his kingdom, they risked everything.

As it was with them, so it should be with us. Alas, in order to avoid colliding with the world, contemporary evangelicals so often accommodate themselves, their churches and the gospel to it; their aim is to attract the world, not confront it, to make the *ekklēsia* as like the world as it can, not to separate from it.[2] But the scriptural call has never been rescinded. Let us remind ourselves of it:

> Do not be unequally yoked with unbelievers. For what partnership has righteousness with lawlessness? Or what fellowship has light with darkness? What accord has Christ with Belial? Or what portion does a believer share with an unbeliever? What agreement has the temple of God with idols? For we are the temple of the living God; as God said: 'I will make my dwelling among them and walk among them, and I will be their God, and they shall be my people. Therefore go out from their midst, and be separate from them, says the Lord, and touch no unclean thing; then I will welcome you, and I will be a father to you, and you shall be sons and daughters to me, says the Lord Almighty' (2 Cor. 6:14-18).

And:

---

became as one under the law (though not being myself under the law) that I might win those under the law. To those outside the law I became as one outside the law (not being outside the law of God but under the law of Christ) that I might win those outside the law. To the weak I became weak, that I might win the weak. I have become all things to all people, that by all means I might save some. I do it all for the sake of the gospel, that I may share with them in its blessings' (1 Cor. 9:19-23). This, however, must not be stretched to become a *carte blanche* justifying compromise of the gospel.

[2] For more on this, see, for instance, my *Relationship*; *To Confront*; *Dilemma*; *Evangelicals Warned*.

Jesus also suffered outside the gate in order to sanctify the people through his own blood. Therefore let us go to him outside the camp and bear the reproach he endured (Heb. 13:12-13).

Do not misread the writer's use of 'let us'. It has all the force of a command – an imperative – combined with the urging of and pleading with his readers (see Heb. 4:1,11,14,16; 6:1; 10:22,23,24; 12:1,28; 13:13,15).[3]

The fact is, none of what we have seen in Scripture about the way the first believers approached the world should be filed under the label 'History – of Academic or Antiquarian Interest Only': it applies today; indeed, it must govern our thinking and practice today. And it is not only that apostolic authority has not changed; two thousand years have passed, and cultures have evolved, but man is still the same as he has ever been since the fall – lost, dead in sin, and implacably opposed to God and his Christ. As it was in the days of the psalmists, so today:

The kings of the earth set themselves, and the rulers take counsel together, against the LORD and against his Anointed, saying: 'Let us burst their bonds apart and cast away their cords from us' (Ps. 2:2-3).

How long, O God, is the foe to scoff? Is the enemy to revile your name forever?... Remember this, O LORD, how the enemy scoffs, and a foolish people reviles your name... Arise, O God, defend your cause; remember how the foolish scoff at you all the day! Do not forget the clamour of your foes, the uproar of those who rise against you, which goes up continually! (Ps. 74:10,18,22-23).

And we have the encouragement, challenge and instruction of the attitude of the early believers when they faced opposition; they turned to such psalms and wielded them in crying to God for power to stand and confront sinners:

When they [that is, Peter and John] were released, they went to their friends and reported what the chief priests and the elders had said to them. And when they heard it, they lifted their

---

[3] See my 'Quit the Camp' on my sermonaudio.com page.

voices together to God and said: 'Sovereign Lord, who made the heaven and the earth and the sea and everything in them', who through the mouth of our father David, your servant, said by the Holy Spirit: "Why did the Gentiles rage, and the peoples plot in vain? The kings of the earth set themselves, and the rulers were gathered together, against the Lord and against his Anointed" – for truly in this city there were gathered together against your holy servant Jesus, whom you anointed, both Herod and Pontius Pilate, along with the Gentiles and the peoples of Israel, to do whatever your hand and your plan had predestined to take place. And now, Lord, look upon their threats and grant to your servants to continue to speak your word with all boldness, while you stretch out your hand to heal, and signs and wonders are performed through the name of your holy servant Jesus'. And when they had prayed, the place in which they were gathered together was shaken, and they were all filled with the Holy Spirit and continued to speak the word of God with boldness (Acts 4:23-31).

I need not labour the point. But I will call upon Spurgeon to make the necessary emphasis. Spurgeon (in a sermon on Romans 2:16 – '...that day when, according to my gospel, God judges the secrets of men by Christ Jesus') spelled out that the gospel speaks, not only of God's love for sinners, but his inevitable wrath upon unbelievers on the day of judgment[4] under Christ:

He that will sit upon the throne as the vice-regent of God, and as a judge, acting for God, will be Jesus Christ. What a name for a judge! The Saviour-Anointed Jesus Christ: he is to be the judge of all mankind. Our Redeemer will be the umpire of our destiny.
This will be, I doubt not, first for the display of his glory. What a difference there will be then between the babe of Bethlehem's manger, hunted by Herod, carried down by night into Egypt for shelter, and the King of kings and Lord of lords, before whom every knee must bow! What a difference between the weary man and full of woes, and he that shall then be girt with glory, sitting on a throne encircled with a rainbow! From the derision of men to the throne of universal judgment, what an ascent! I am unable to convey to you my own heart's sense

---

[4] Sinners are already under the wrath of God (John 3:36).

of the contrast between the 'despised and rejected of men', and the universally-acknowledged Lord, before whom Caesars and pontiffs shall bow into the dust. He who was judged at Pilate's bar, shall summon all to his bar. What a change from the shame and spitting, from the nails and the wounds, the mockery and the thirst, and the dying anguish, to the glory in which he shall come whose eyes are as a flame of fire, and out of whose mouth there goes a two-edged sword! He shall judge the nations, even he whom the nations abhorred. He shall break them in pieces like a potter's vessel, even those who cast him out as unworthy to live among them. Oh, how we ought to bow before him now as he reveals himself in his tender sympathy, and in his generous humiliation! Let us kiss the Son lest he be angry; let us yield to his grace, that we may not be crushed by his wrath. You sinners, bow before those pierced feet, which else will tread you like clusters in the wine-press. Look up to him with weeping, and confess your forgetfulness of him, and put your trust in him; lest he look down on you in indignation. Oh, remember that he will one day say: 'But those mine enemies, which would not that I should reign over them, bring hither, and slay them before me'. The holding of the judgment by the Lord Jesus will greatly enhance his glory. It will finally settle one controversy which is still upheld by certain erroneous spirits: there will be no doubt about our Lord's deity in that day: there will be no question that this same Jesus who was crucified is both Lord and God. God himself shall judge, but he shall perform the judgment in the person of his Son Jesus Christ, truly man, but nevertheless most truly God. Being God he is divinely qualified to judge the world in righteousness, and the people with his truth.

If you ask again, Why is the Son of God chosen to be the final judge? I could give as a further answer that he receives this high office not only as a reward for all his pains, and as a manifestation of his glory, but also because [believing] men have been under his mediatorial sway, and he is their Governor and King. At the present moment we are all under the sway of the Prince Immanuel, God with us: we have been placed by an act of divine clemency, not under the immediate government of an offended God, but under the reconciling rule of the Prince of Peace. 'All power is given unto him in heaven and in earth'. 'The Father judges no man, but has committed all judgment unto the Son: that all men should honour the Son, even as they honour the Father'. We are commanded to preach unto the

people, and 'to testify that it is he which was ordained of God
to be the judge of quick and dead' (Acts 10:42)...
'According to my gospel', says Paul; and he meant that the
judgment is an essential part of the gospel creed.

I break in. This is the material point which must be grasped,
stressed, and acted on today: yes, God in the gospel reveals his
love for sinners, but if, in our preaching, we do not give biblical
weight to God's wrath, we do not preach the gospel – we preach
another gospel, which is no gospel at all (Gal. 1:6-7).

Spurgeon continued:

If I had to sum up the gospel I should have to tell you certain
facts: Jesus, the Son of God, became man; he was born of the
virgin Mary; lived a perfect life; was falsely accused of men;
was crucified, dead, and buried; the third day he rose again
from the dead; he ascended into heaven and sits on the right
hand of God; from whence he shall also come to judge the
quick and the dead. This is one of the elementary truths of our
gospel; we believe in the resurrection of the dead, the final
judgment, and the life everlasting.
The judgment is according to our gospel, and in times of
righteous indignation its terrible significance seems a very
gospel to the pure in heart. I mean this. I have read this and that
concerning oppression, slavery, the treading down of the poor,
and the shedding of blood, and I have rejoiced that there is a
righteous judge... It has come like a gospel to us that the Lord
will be revealed in flaming fire, taking vengeance on them that
know not God, and that obey not the gospel of our Lord Jesus
Christ (2 Thess. 1:8) The secret wickedness of the world[5]
cannot go on for ever. Even they that love men best, and most
desire salvation for them, cannot but cry to God: 'How long!
How long! Great God, will you for ever endure this?' God has
appointed a day in which he will judge the world, and we sigh
and cry until it shall end the reign of wickedness, and give rest
to the oppressed.[6]

---

[5] Original 'London'.

[6] This note is muted today. But not in Scripture.
'They sing the song of Moses, the servant of God, and the song of the
Lamb, saying: "Great and amazing are your deeds, O Lord God the
Almighty! Just and true are your ways, O King of the nations! Who

Now for punch line:

Brethren, we must preach the coming of the Lord, and preach it somewhat more than we have done; because it is the driving power of the gospel. Too many have kept back these truths, and thus the bone has been taken out of the arm of the gospel. Its point has been broken; its edge has been blunted. The doctrine of judgment to come is the power by which men are to be aroused. There is another life; the Lord will come a second time; judgment will arrive; the wrath of God will be revealed. Where this is not preached, I am bold to say the gospel is not preached. It is absolutely necessary to the preaching of the gospel of Christ that men be warned as to what will happen if they continue in their sins. Ho, ho, sir surgeon, you are too delicate to tell the man that he is ill! You hope to heal the sick without their knowing it. You therefore flatter them; and what happens? They laugh at you; they dance upon their own graves. At last they die! Your delicacy is cruelty; your flatteries are poisons; you are a murderer. Shall we keep men in a fool's paradise? Shall we lull them into soft slumbers from which they will awake in hell? Are we to become helpers of their damnation by our smooth speeches? In the name of God we will not. It becomes every true minister of Christ to cry aloud and spare not, for God has set a day in which he will 'judge the secrets of men by Jesus Christ according to my gospel'. As surely as Paul's gospel was true the judgment will come.

---

will not fear, O Lord, and glorify your name? For you alone are holy. All nations will come and worship you, for your righteous acts [that is, your judgments] have been revealed"' (Rev. 15:3-4).

'I heard the angel in charge of the waters say: "Just are you, O Holy One, who is and who was, for you brought these judgments. For they have shed the blood of saints and prophets, and you have given them blood to drink. It is what they deserve!" I heard the altar saying: "Yes, Lord God the Almighty, true and just are your judgments!"' (Rev. 16:5-7).

'I heard what seemed to be the loud voice of a great multitude in heaven, crying out: "Hallelujah! Salvation and glory and power belong to our God, for his judgments are true and just; for he has judged the great prostitute who corrupted the earth with her immorality, and has avenged on her the blood of his servants". Once more they cried out: "Hallelujah! The smoke from her goes up forever and ever"' (Rev. 19:1-3).

Wherefore flee to Jesus this day, O sinners. O you saints, come hide yourselves again beneath the crimson canopy of the atoning sacrifice, that you may be now ready to welcome your descending Lord and escort him to his judgment-seat. O my hearers, may God bless you, for Jesus' sake. Amen.[7]

The preaching of the coming Christ as King, the resurrection of all the dead to judgment, and the establishing of the kingdom in all its fullness – sinners must hear this!

Consecration

I cannot do better than repeat Paul's words to the Colossians:

[Since] then you have been raised with Christ, seek the things that are above, where Christ is, seated at the right hand of God. Set your minds on things that are above, not on things that are on earth. For you have died, and your life is hidden with Christ in God. When Christ who is your life appears, then you also will appear with him in glory. Put to death therefore what is earthly in you... seeing that you have put off the old self with its practices and have put on the new self, which is being renewed in knowledge after the image of its creator. Here there is not Greek and Jew, circumcised and uncircumcised, barbarian, Scythian, slave, free; but Christ is all, and in all (Col. 3:1-11).

That says it all!

---

[7] C.H.Spurgeon sermon 1849, 'Coming Judgment of the Secrets of Men', on Rom. 2:16.

Comfort

Judging by what Scripture says of the first believers' attitude to suffering, bereavement and death, the focus of the believer's comfort or consolation – scripturally speaking – in face of such seeming calamities and sorrows, has to be Christ's return, the believer's resurrection and entrance into the everlasting kingdom of Christ. It is not the believer's death and joys of the intermediate state; nor is it the establishment of a glorious kingdom before Christ's return. The first of these two false alternatives has been prevalent for centuries; as we have seen, the second, alas, is gaining more and more of a foothold among evangelicals.

I will not repeat my arguments here. I simply urge that we (and I include myself) should retrace our steps and, as in the extract from Colossians 3, set our minds on Christ and his appearing. That's the positive. As for the negative, let us give up sentimental speculation about the intermediate state, and rid ourselves of pipe-dreams of an earthly utopia (or something near it) *before* Christ's return.

As Calvin put it when speaking about the intermediate state (but his words are equally applicable to post-millennial dreams):

> To pry curiously into their intermediate state is neither lawful nor expedient... It is foolish and rash to inquire into hidden things, farther than God permits us to know... What teacher or doctor will reveal to us what God has concealed?... Since Scripture uniformly enjoins us to look with expectation to the [second] advent of Christ, and delays the crown of glory till that period, let us be contented with the limits divinely prescribed to us – that is, that the souls of the righteous, after their warfare is ended, obtain blessed rest where in joy they wait for the fruition of promised glory, and that thus the final result is suspended till Christ the Redeemer appears. There can be no doubt that the reprobate have the same doom as that which Jude assigns to the devils, they are 'reserved in everlasting chains under darkness unto the judgment of the great day' (Jude 6).[8]

---

[8] John Calvin: *Institutes of the Christian Religion* 3.25.6.

But let me not finish with Calvin; let me remind you of the believer's hope when facing death, and doing so by quoting the words of Paul to the grieving and anxious believers at Thessalonica:

> We do not want you to be uninformed, brothers, about those who are asleep [that is, those believers who have died], that you may not grieve as others do who have no hope. For since we believe that Jesus died and rose again, even so, through Jesus, God will bring with him those who have fallen asleep. For this we declare to you by a word from the Lord, that we who are alive, who are left until the coming of the Lord, will not precede those who have fallen asleep. For the Lord himself will descend from heaven with a cry of command, with the voice of an archangel, and with the sound of the trumpet of God. And the dead in Christ will rise first. Then we who are alive, who are left, will be caught up together with them in the clouds to meet the Lord in the air, and so we will always be with the Lord. Therefore encourage one another with these words (1 Thess. 4:13-18).

May it be said of every reader of these pages:

> Through the Spirit, by faith, we ourselves eagerly wait for the hope of righteousness (Gal. 5:5).

And that is the return of Christ, the resurrection and the bringing in of the kingdom.

APPENDICES

Appendix 1
A Brief Reply to Post-Millennialism

More specifically, in this Appendix I want to make a brief reply to the claims of Sharon James in her books *How Christianity Transformed the World*, Christian Focus Publications, Fearn, 2021 and *The Lies We Are Told...*, Christian Focus Publications, Fearn, 2022. This reply, though brief, proved too large for a footnote; hence this Appendix. It is not, it goes without saying, a full rebuttal of post-millennialism.[1]

James argues for post-millennialism based on old-covenant texts, heyday-Puritan prophetical dreams (ignoring late Puritans who had to live with defeat), Jonathan Edwards, selective C.H.Spurgeon, and (very heavily) on Iain Murray: *The Puritan Hope*, Banner of Truth Trust, Edinburgh, 1971.

My reply:

A golden kingdom before Christ's return? What about the overwhelming weight of the New Testament which gives powerful evidence of serious declension in churches even during apostolic times, and warns of inevitable apostasy throughout this age, intensifying at its end? For the former, read 1 Corinthians, Galatians, Hebrews and Revelation 2 & 3, just for starters, and compare Paul's letter to the Ephesians with Revelation 2:1-7! For the latter, see, for example, Matthew 24; Luke 17:26-30; 1 Thessalonians 5:2-4; 2 Thessalonians 2:1-12; 1 Timothy 4:1-5; 2 Timothy 3:1-12; 2 Peter 3; *etc., etc.* Take Israel's appalling record of declension in the days of the old covenant; as for the history of Christendom! All this speaks volumes.

This is a very serious matter; it is not just a technical point for prophetical buffs to chew over. False kingdom hopes can cause

---

[1] For more, see my *Romans 11*.

serious spiritual damage to those who hold them. Take the 1640s (see my *Battle*). Millennial schemes (of whatever sort) appear to allow that the glorious earthly kingdom which they expect will collapse just before Christ's (final) return. How does that fit with: 'Let us be grateful for receiving a kingdom that cannot be shaken' (Heb. 12:8)? Are there two kingdoms – one which can be shaken, the other not? 'Here we have no lasting city, but we seek the city that is to come' (Heb. 13:14).

As for Spurgeon, I admit his inconstancy over the question. But consider this from late Spurgeon (preaching on 2 Timothy 3:5 in 1889):

> There are sanguine brothers and sisters who are looking forward to everything growing better and better and better, until, at last, this present age ripens into a millennium. They will not be able to sustain their hopes, for Scripture gives them no solid basis to rest upon. We who believe that there will be no millennial reign[2] without the King and who expect no rule of righteousness except from the appearing of the righteous Lord, are nearer the mark. Apart from the second advent of our Lord, the world is more likely to sink into a pandemonium than to rise into a millennium. A divine interposition seems to me the hope set before us in Scripture and, indeed, to be the only hope adequate to the occasion. We look to the darkening down of things. The state of mankind, however improved politically, may yet grow worse and worse spiritually. Certainly, we are assured... that 'evil men and seducers shall wax worse and worse, deceiving and being deceived'. There will spring up in the... church and round about it, a body of faithless men who profess to have faith – ungodly men who will unite with the saints – men having the form of godliness but denying the power. We may call these hard times [that is, 1889], if we will, but we have hardly yet come to the border of those truly harder times when it will go hard with the church and she shall need, even more than today, to cry mightily unto the Lord to keep her alive.[3]

---

[2] The kingdom will not be for a 1000 years; it is eternal (Dan. 7:14,27; Luke 1:31-33; 2 Pet. 1:11; Rev. 11:15).

[3] C.H.Spurgeon sermon 2088.

Appendix 2
A Look at Luke 23:43

In publishing this Appendix I know that I am playing with fire. For some, it will, once and for all, prove that my works should be avoided. I am a dangerous man, not to say verging on being a heretic. This Appendix will be the last straw.[1]

On the other hand, for a few – almost certainly, only a *very* few – it might be that reading these pages might prove to be a blessing, an eye-opener, something which might, for them, shed new light on a well-known and frequently-preached passage. It might remind them how many evangelicals have allowed one of the great truths of the new covenant to slip through their fingers. Furthermore, it might help them to see how Christ was magnificently glorified from a most unexpected quarter at what seemed to be his lowest point. (Do not miss my deliberate, repeated use of 'might' in all that!). Anyway, the writing of this book (this Appendix in particular) has done all that for me.

What's in a comma?

Commas can be troublesome things, very troublesome things.

A woman had recently been bereaved. Writing to a friend, she said: 'My husband died last week, what awful weather we've been having'. Think of the weight that poor comma had to carry!

Oscar Wilde, wishing (I strongly suspect) to deflate a pompous enquirer who had asked how he'd spent his day, replied to the effect that for half of it he'd been toying with inserting a comma in a poem, and for the other half taking it out.

---

[1] To add another cliché: it will put the tin hat on it.

And what about Sir Roger Casement – the man who 'was hanged on a comma'? Well... no, actually, he wasn't; it would be more accurate to say he was hanged on the absence of a comma – or, at least, on the doubt as to whether a smudge on an old manuscript was – or was not – a comma. What a difference that made!

This is how it came about.

During the First World War I, Casement was charged with violating the Treason Act of 1351 by trying to raise German support for the Easter Rising in Ireland.[2] Casement's counsel, not denying the facts, argued that because of the punctuation – or lack of it – in the original (medieval) legal document, his client was not technically guilty of treason. After detailed scrutiny of the ancient manuscript by learnèd legal men, Casement was found guilty and hanged; hence, hanged on a comma (or its absence).

Yes, commas can be troublesome things.

Consider this:

Bill rode on his horse sweating profusely.

Should we understand that Bill needed a shower:

Bill rode on his horse, sweating profusely?

Or that Bill's nag needed a good rub down:

Bill rode on, his horse sweating profusely?

---

[2] The Easter Rising, also known as the Easter Rebellion, was an armed insurrection in Ireland in April 1916. Some Irish nationalists proclaimed an Irish Republic and, along with some 1,600 followers, seized prominent buildings in Dublin, thereby coming into conflict with British troops. Within a week, the insurrection had been quashed, with more than 2,000 dead or injured. The leaders of the rebellion were executed, but, with the passage of time, they came to be regarded as martyrs. In 1921, a treaty was signed, establishing the Irish Free State in 1922. Hence, the modern-day Republic of Ireland.

All very interesting no doubt – perhaps amusing – but why am I spending time on a comma? A comma, I ask you! Talk about a storm in a teacup! It won't be long before I'll be arguing about angels and pinheads.

Not so fast!

A comma may be a very small mark on a page, but, as we have seen, it can carry a very heavy weight and have far-reaching consequences.

Moreover, I am concerned about a certain comma we find in the Bible. Specifically, I want to take another look[3] at the comma in Luke's record of the interchange between Christ and one of the two criminals at the crucifixion. Here are the key words:

> [Jesus] said to [the thief] : 'Truly, I say to you, today you will be with me in paradise' (Luke 23:43).

Or... and here comes the crunch... should it be:

> [Jesus] said to [the thief] : 'Truly, I say to you today, you will be with me in paradise' (Luke 23:43)?

Oh no! What a fuss about nothing! 'Tis only a comma after all. But, as the section heading says, what's in a comma? Read on!

But before you do, let me point out that this is not an isolated incident. Consider Isaiah 40:1. Is it a command to the prophet:

> Comfort my people.

Or an encouragement to Israel:

> Comfort [that is, take comfort], my people?

It's all in the comma!

The placing of the comma

I can imagine it: 'What's all the fuss about? Why the doubt? My Bible has the comma after "say"; so does virtually every other

---

[3] Many people have thought about the issue and produced much on it.

version. That's good enough for me. Jesus was assuring the thief that he would – on that very day – be with him in paradise. Done and dusted!'

So most might confidently say. End of story!

But we have to be more mature than that! Big – and I mean big – questions are involved.

The fact is, Luke put no comma at all. Indeed, the original New Testament was written in continuous text, with no gaps between words, and all in small or upper case! Something like this – but in Greek, of course:

ISAYTOYOUTODAYYOUWILLBEWITHMEIN
PARADISE

Or:

isaytoyoutodayyouwillbewithmeinparadise

All punctuation marks in Scripture are simply translators' suggestions to aid our understanding. They might be right; they might be wrong. It is the same with the division of the Bible into chapters and verses; none of the sacred writers did anything of the sort. Centuries after the canon of Scripture was complete, some well-meaning men thought it would be a good idea to break the text into chapters and then into verses – with the aim of making it easier to navigate one's way round the Bible.[4] Sadly, these imposed divisions often cloud the meaning of the text. So much so, I digress to strongly advise all Bible readers, whatever version they use, to use a paragraph Bible. While this does not get rid of all the difficulties – the translators and printers still have to decide on paragraph breaks – at least the difficulties are reduced.

What should we do? What can we do? Should we just accept the translators' opinion – the translators know best? Or should we

---

[4] Stephen Langton introduced chapters in the 13th century, and Robert Estienne (Stephanas) introduced verses in the 16th century. Rome uses a slightly different arrangement.

trust Mother – Mother, being, as the Church Father, Cyprian (and, following him, Rome and most of the Reformed from Calvin on), would tell us – being the Church: the Church tells us! But... which Church?

In any case, if we go down that route it signals the end of all argument – and more: it signals the end of all thought! Indeed, we have stepped right back into the medieval – the Dark Ages, in fact – when the Church told the faithful – the gullible – what to believe.

Who wants to go there?

Let's get back to the nub of the question, and look at the interchange between Christ and the two criminals at the crucifixion. Here is the full account:

> Two others, who were criminals, were led away to be put to death with [Christ]. And when they came to the place that is called 'The Skull', there they crucified him, and the criminals, one on his right and one on his left. And Jesus said: 'Father, forgive them, for they know not what they do'. And they cast lots to divide his garments. And the people stood by, watching, but the rulers scoffed at him, saying: 'He saved others; let him save himself, if he is the Christ of God, his Chosen One!'. The soldiers also mocked him, coming up and offering him sour wine and saying: 'If you are the King of the Jews, save yourself!' There was also an inscription over him: 'This is the King of the Jews'.
> One of the criminals who were hanged railed at him, saying: 'Are you not the Christ? Save yourself and us!' But the other rebuked him, saying, 'Do you not fear God, since you are under the same sentence of condemnation? And we indeed justly, for we are receiving the due reward of our deeds; but this man has done nothing wrong'. And he said: 'Jesus, remember me when you come into your kingdom'. And he said to him: 'Truly, I say to you today, you will be with me in paradise' (Luke 23:32-43).

Leaving out the questionable punctuation, the key words are:

> Truly, I say to you today you will be with me in paradise.

As for 'paradise', I believe it is a reference to heaven (2 Cor. 12:2-3; Rev. 2:7) (or, in the context, bliss in the kingdom), but that is not the issue I wish to deal with. It is the placing of that comma that is all important in this present discussion.

Clearly:

> I say to you, today you will be with me in paradise...

...is very different to:

> I say to you today, you will be with me in paradise.

Now, as for that comma in Luke 23:43, unless we are going to blindly accept the translators' opinion, or Mother Church and her theologians' opinions, we have to decide on other grounds. Ah! But what grounds? Principally, context and biblical usage.

I assert that on both grounds – context and biblical usage – there is good reason to argue that the comma should be placed thus:

> I say to you today, you will be with me in paradise.

In saying this, I admit that I am running counter to the traditional rendering of the verse in almost all versions and accepted evangelical-theology, and, as a result, as I have said, I will almost certainly be marked as a heretic.[5]

As for the traditional view, take John Gill who, in his *Commentary*, left nobody in any doubt where he stood; he certainly showed he was no fan of putting the comma after 'today':

> Besides it being senseless, and impertinent, and only contrived to serve an hypothesis, is not agreeable to Christ's usual way of speaking, and contrary to all copies and versions.

Phew! Indeed, Gill dismissed what I might call 'my' placing of the comma and 'my' reasons for it as 'this silly criticism'.

---

[5] I also acknowledge that it is the version favoured by the Jehovah Witnesses with their New World Translation, but that does not of necessity mean that it is wrong. Not a few evangelical scholars – not least, E.W.Bullinger – have favoured it.

So now you know! Hence my health warning.

My point at this stage is simple: since Luke used no punctuation, then at the very least – at the very least, I say – we should be cautious about inserting punctuation. *Tradition must not be our guide! Nor must fear – fear of being ostracised for daring to take a non-traditional line!* The same goes for basing one's view on a theological system, however revered, however hoary. Such systems, such Confessions, are all man-made, drawn up to deal with contemporary problems troubling believers often centuries ago, and can be riddled with Christendom-political overtones.[6] We must be guided by scriptural context and scriptural usage.

A vital negative

Before I plunge myself even more deeply into even hotter water, let me state it as clearly as I can that I am not calling into question the traditional view of the believer's blessed state after death.[7] I cautiously – note the word, since there is a huge amount of speculation foisted upon Scripture on this issue – I cautiously believe that the believer at death is taken to be with Christ, and nothing that I say here inflicts the slightest damage

---

[6] *The Westminster Confession of Faith* and its Catechisms are no exception. One of Parliament's main concerns was to eliminate what they considered to be antinomianism. Hence the legal tone of the Confession with its heavy emphasis on the law, following Calvin. See, for instance, my 'The Law and The Confessions'.

[7] I frankly admit that this section must give the impression that I want it both ways. Not really. I am convinced the balance should come down on the last day, and the coming of the kingdom. As Calvin said – see above – 'To pry curiously into their intermediate state is neither lawful nor expedient... It is foolish and rash to inquire into hidden things, farther than God permits us to know'. John Piper: 'Our judgment will be after we die... Heb. 9:27 makes it explicit... We don't need to be more specific than that this morning. We need only say that before we enter the final state of glory with our resurrection bodies on the new earth, we will stand before Christ as Judge' (John Piper: 'What Happens When You Die? All Appear Before the Judgment Seat of Christ', a sermon preached 1st Aug. 1993).

on that. The believer, after death, is with Christ; death does not, in any way, interrupt his communion with his Saviour; indeed, death actually enhances it:

> I am sure that neither death nor life, nor angels nor rulers, nor things present nor things to come, nor powers, nor height nor depth, nor anything else in all creation, will be able to separate us from the love of God in Christ Jesus our Lord (Rom. 8:38-39).

We know that if the tent that is our earthly home is destroyed, we have a building from God, a house not made with hands, eternal in the heavens. For in this tent we groan, longing to put on our heavenly dwelling, if indeed by putting it on we may not be found naked. For while we are still in this tent, we groan, being burdened – not that we would be unclothed, but that we would be further clothed, so that what is mortal may be swallowed up by life. He who has prepared us for this very thing is God, who has given us the Spirit as a guarantee. So we are always of good courage. We know that while we are at home in the body we are away from the Lord, for we walk by faith, not by sight. Yes, we are of good courage, and we would rather be away from the body and at home with the Lord (2 Cor. 5:1-8).[8]

If we live, we live to the Lord, and if we die, we die to the Lord. So then, whether we live or whether we die, we are the Lord's. For to this end Christ died and lived again, that he might be Lord both of the dead and of the living (Rom. 14:8-9).

My eager expectation and hope that I will not be at all ashamed, but that with full courage now as always Christ will be honoured in my body, whether by life or by death. For to me to live is Christ, and to die is gain. If I am to live in the flesh, that means fruitful labour for me. Yet which I shall choose I cannot tell. I am hard pressed between the two. My desire is to depart and be with Christ, for that is far better (Phil. 1:20-23).

God has not destined us for wrath, but to obtain salvation through our Lord Jesus Christ, who died for us so that whether

---

[8] The believer gets his resurrected body – obviously – at the resurrection, at Christ's return (John 5:25,28; 11:24; 1 Cor. 15:22-23; Phil. 3:20-21). See, in the main text, the relevant note on this point.

we are awake or asleep [that is, live or die] we might live with him. Therefore encourage one another and build one another up, just as you are doing (1 Thess. 5:9-11).

You have come to Mount Zion and to the city of the living God, the heavenly Jerusalem, and to innumerable angels in festal gathering, and to the assembly of the firstborn who are enrolled in heaven, and to God, the judge of all, and to the spirits of the righteous made perfect, and to Jesus, the mediator of a new covenant, and to the sprinkled blood that speaks a better word than the blood of Abel (Heb. 12:22-24).

I will never leave you nor forsake you (Heb. 13:5).

These passages, in my view, teach that death in no way interrupts the believer's communion with Christ. I know that some believers take a different view about these verses, but I stick (as I say, cautiously) with what might be called the traditional or orthodox view. Consequently, I am not going to argue the case for the blessed condition of the believing dead; this is not the point at issue here. *But neither is it the point in Luke 23:43. **And that IS my point!***

So... if this caveat is understood and accepted – even though I am questioning the placing of a comma in Luke 23:43, I am not calling into question the blessed condition of the believing dead – let us go on.

Problems for the traditional view

Those who take the traditional view of Luke 23:43 – that the verse teaches that Christ was telling the thief that he would that very day be in paradise with Christ – have one or two problems they need to face up to.

Take Hebrews 9:27:

It is appointed for man to die once, and after that comes judgment.

Was the thief judged immediately following death, and then immediately entered paradise with Christ? This surely presents a problem for the traditional view – which theologians and commentators who hold that view seem often either to avoid or feel able to 'solve'. Take Gill:

> There is a particular judgment which is immediately after death; by virtue of which, the souls of men are condemned to their proper state of happiness or woe; and there is an universal judgment, which will be after the resurrection of the dead, and is called eternal judgment, and to come; this is appointed by God, though the time when [it is to take place] is unknown to men; yet nothing is more certain, and it will be a righteous one.

As can be seen, Gill has asserted that the believer undergoes two judgments – which he called particular and general – the first immediately following his death, and the second when Christ returns. Very well! But do not miss the complete absence of scriptural evidence for this confident assertion – for that is what it is: a confident assertion of a man's opinion. You can either take Gill's pontification, or...?

Albert Barnes was of the same opinion, again entirely without scriptural warrant. Indeed, he frankly admitted his view was nothing more than a 'supposition':

> The [writer] does not say 'how long' after death this [judgment] will be, nor is it possible for us to know... We may suppose, however, that there will be two periods in which there will be an act of judgment passed on those who die.

Let me not be misunderstood. I am not saying Gill or Barnes were wrong.[9] I just do not know. Nor does anybody else. But Hebrews 9:27 lends no support to the view that believers, at death, are judged, pronounced righteous, and enter into everlasting bliss (only to be subjected to a repeat of the process of judgment, *etc.* at the return of Christ). Let me remind you of the verse:

> It is appointed for man to die once, and after that comes judgment.

---

[9] See above for the extract from Calvin where he showed that he accepted that there was a separation between the godly and the ungodly at death.

After death comes the judgment – immediately or at Christ's return? That is one problem for the traditional placing of the comma.

Here's another. If Luke 23:43 does mean that Christ (and the thief) entered paradise that very day, why did Christ say to Mary on the resurrection morning: 'Do not cling to me, for I have not yet ascended to the Father' (John 20:17)?

Oh, I know that theologians, commentators and preachers will have their explanations, but such explanations need very strong scriptural justification. Do they get it?

Starting with the Church Fathers, continuing down to the present day, a huge edifice of speculation has been constructed on Luke 23:43 – much of it of the angels-on-a pinhead variety.[10]

Let me leave the negative and come to the positive.

* * *

What if the comma is placed thus:

I say to you today, you will be with me in paradise.

Doesn't this make Christ guilty of a pleonasm[11] – as critics suggest? Not at all. In justifying this punctuation, I spoke of context and scriptural usage. The context, as I have shown, overwhelmingly supports the comma after 'today'. But before I get to that, we need to ask if there is any scriptural warrant for it?

There certainly is! Consider:

---

[10] Because he held to baptismal regeneration (see my *Infant*), Augustine wavered about whether or not the thief was sprinkled by the bodily fluids flowing from Christ, and the difference – or otherwise – that this made. I do not mention this to excite curiosity, but to serve as a warning to those who want either to speculate or to make biblical text fit a presupposed theology or confession. Theologians can always come up with a convenient 'solution' to any problem!

[11] That is, a redundancy, using more words than necessary, padding, waffle.

I call heaven and earth to witness against you *today* (Deut. 4:26).

These words that I command you *today* shall be on your heart (Deut. 6:6).

I solemnly warn you *today* that you shall surely perish (Deut. 8:19).

You shall therefore be careful to do the commandment and the statutes and the rules that I command you *today* (Deut. 7:11).

See, I am setting before you *today* a blessing and a curse (Deut. 11:26).

The LORD will make you the head and not the tail, and you shall only go up and not down, if you obey the commandments of the LORD your God, which I command you *today*, being careful to do them, and if you do not turn aside from any of the words that I command you *today*, to the right hand or to the left, to go after other gods to serve them (Deut. 28:13-14).

See, I have set before you *today* life and good, death and evil. If you obey the commandments of the LORD your God that I command you *today*... I declare to you *today*... I call heaven and earth to witness against you *today*, that I have set before you life and death, blessing and curse (Deut. 30:15-19).

Take to heart all the words by which I am warning you *today* (Deut. 32:46).

Therefore I testify to you *this day* that I am innocent of the blood of all (Acts 20:26).

I am going to make my defence *today* (Acts 26:2).

In all these cases, the 'today' could be omitted, and the sense would be unimpaired – except... and this is the point... the use of the 'today' gives a powerful sense of urgency, drawing attention to the present circumstances in which the words were uttered.

And that is the cardinal point about Luke 23:43. We are talking about the thief's confession, and Christ's endorsement of it, on that day of appalling darkness and seeming defeat.

So I repeat: the criticism levelled against this punctuation – that it makes Christ guilty of a pleonasm – is dealt with at a stroke; there is nothing 'mere' about the proper punctuation.

While I freely acknowledge that Spurgeon agreed with the traditional punctuation, and while he certainly thought that when Christ spoke of 'today' he meant that the thief would be in heaven with Christ that very day, nevertheless, he also got the point I have been making, and he expressed it in his usual memorable style:

> Remember, beloved friends, that our Lord Jesus, at the time he saved this malefactor, was at his lowest. His glory had been ebbing out in Gethsemane, and before Caiaphas, and Herod, and Pilate; but it had now reached the utmost low-water mark. Stripped of his garments, and nailed to the cross, our Lord was mocked by a ribald crowd, and was dying in agony: then was he 'numbered with the transgressors', and made as the offscouring of all things. Yet, while in that condition, he achieved this marvellous deed of grace. Behold the wonder wrought by the Saviour when emptied of all his glory, and hanged up a spectacle of shame upon the brink of death! How certain is it that he can do great wonders of mercy now, seeing that he has returned unto his glory, and sits upon the throne of light! 'He is able to save them to the uttermost that come unto God by him, seeing he ever lives to make intercession for them' [Heb. 7:25]...
>
> It is not only the weakness of our Lord which makes the salvation of the penitent thief memorable; it is the fact that the dying malefactor saw it before his very eyes. Can you put yourself into his place, and suppose yourself to be looking upon one who hangs in agony upon a cross? Could you readily believe him to be the Lord of glory, who would soon come to his kingdom? That was no mean faith which, at such a moment, could believe in Jesus as Lord and King... [Think of the] remarkable faith with [which] this thief, who believed in a crucified, derided and dying Christ, and cried to him as to one whose kingdom would surely come. The thief's faith was the more remarkable because he was himself in great pain, and bound to die. It is not easy to exercise confidence when you are tortured with deadly anguish. Our own rest of mind has at times been greatly hindered by pain of body. When we are the subjects of acute suffering it is not easy to exhibit that faith

which we fancy we possess at other times. This man, suffering as he did, and seeing the Saviour in so sad a state, nevertheless believed unto life eternal. Herein was such faith as is seldom seen.

Recollect, also, that he was surrounded by scoffers. It is easy to swim with the current, and hard to go against the stream. This man heard the priests, in their pride, ridicule the Lord, and the great multitude of the common people, with one consent, joined in the scorning; his comrade caught the spirit of the hour, and mocked also, and perhaps he did the same for a while; but through the grace of God he was changed, and believed in the Lord Jesus in the teeth of all the scorn. His faith was not affected by his surroundings; but he, dying thief as he was, made sure his confidence. Like a jutting rock, standing out in the midst of a torrent, he declared the innocence of the Christ whom others blasphemed. His faith is worthy of our imitation in its fruits. He had no member that was free except his tongue, and he used that member wisely to rebuke his brother malefactor, and defend his Lord. His faith brought forth a brave testimony and a bold confession. I am not going to praise the thief, or his faith, but to extol the glory of that grace divine which gave the thief such faith, and then freely saved him by its means. I am anxious to show how glorious is the Saviour – that Saviour to the uttermost, who, at such a time, could save such a man, and give him so great a faith, and so perfectly and speedily prepare him for eternal bliss. Behold the power of that divine Spirit who could produce such faith on soil so unlikely, and in a climate so unpropitious.[12]

* * *

I have not been word spinning. Vital – eternal – issues hang on what I have been writing about. Reader, you are either a believer or an unbeliever; in biblical terms, you are a saint or a sinner.[13] Whichever you are, Luke's account of the interchange between the dying thief and Christ says things you need to hear. Will you listen?

First, it displays the sovereignty of God: man designs his worst, but God uses that worst to work his best. The Jews clinically

---

[12] C.H.Spurgeon sermon 2078.
[13] All men are born sinners; the redeemed are saints. See my *Man*.

planned the extermination of Christ (Mark 14:1-2,10-11; John 11:46-53; Acts 3:13-15; 7:52), doing the work by Roman hands (Acts 2:23), but God turned their evil machinations gloriously to bring about his eternal purpose. The cross – far from being the ultimate humiliation for Christ, his annihilation, and the end of all he stood for – was made by God, as he had determined before the foundation of the world (Luke 22:22; Acts 2:23; 3:18; 4:27-28; Rom. 16:25; Eph. 1:3-10; 2 Tim. 1:8-10; Tit. 1:1-3; 1 Pet. 1:20) to serve as Christ's throne, his pulpit and his glory. Surveying the cross, this is what the children of God see, rejoice in, and proclaim to the world (1 Cor. 2:2; Gal. 6:14); such is the wonder of Christ's crucifixion. The prophets, those who predicted it, 'searched and enquired carefully' into it, and even angels 'long to look' into it (1 Pet. 1:10-12). What does the cross mean to you?

As to God turning man's evil design to accomplish his purpose, the psalmist set the tone:

> Why do the nations rage and the peoples plot in vain? The kings of the earth set themselves, and the rulers take counsel together, against the LORD and against his Anointed, saying: 'Let us burst their bonds apart and cast away their cords from us'. He who sits in the heavens laughs; the LORD holds them in derision. Then he will speak to them in his wrath, and terrify them in his fury, saying: 'As for me, I have set my king on Zion, my holy hill' (Ps. 2:1-6)...

...bringing his psalm to this conclusion:

> Kiss the Son lest he be angry, and you perish in the way, for his wrath is quickly kindled. Blessed are all who take refuge in him (Ps. 2:12).

Thus the event recorded in Luke 23:36-43, and the proper response to it, was revealed in prophecy through the psalmist!

Secondly, the thief's address to Christ points us to the nature of true faith. Under the most appalling circumstances, even on the darkest of all dark days, against all the external evidence, surrounded by a taunting, hostile mob, the thief penetrated the gloom, pierced the darkness, and was persuaded that Christ is

King. And he appealed to Christ to receive him into his kingdom. What about you?

Thirdly, the thief does more than serve as a signpost pointing you to faith; he challenges you. Can you not hear him say: 'Are you not encouraged to believe, to trust Christ, to submit to him as King – you, with all your advantages? You have far, far more than ever I had: you have the full canon of Scripture; you have an abundance of clear gospel commands, promises, encouragements and warnings; you, almost certainly, have seen and heard abundant personal testimony from believers as to their felt experience of the Lord Jesus Christ. Will this not move you to trust the Saviour for yourself?'

Reader, there is a clear warning here. If I may accommodate the words of Christ[14] in Matthew 12:41-42 to the case in hand:

> The dying thief will rise up at the judgment with this generation and condemn it, for – even in that dire day, at that dreadful time, under those appalling circumstances – he saw Christ as king, one who had a kingdom, confessed it, and wanted to be in it, and yet many, today, even though they have had far greater evidence, think nothing of Christ.

Let me be even more direct, and address every unbeliever reading these words, doing so personally:

> The dying thief will rise up at the judgment with you and condemn you, for – even in that dire day, at that dreadful time, under those appalling circumstances – he saw Christ as king, one who had a kingdom, confessed it, and wanted to be in it, and yet you, today, even though you have had far greater evidence, think nothing of Christ.

Fourthly, the thief's experience exalts God's sovereign grace, and holds out hope to all, especially those who feel themselves

---

[14] 'The men of Nineveh will rise up at the judgment with this generation and condemn it, for they repented at the preaching of Jonah, and behold, something greater than Jonah is here. The queen of the South will rise up at the judgment with this generation and condemn it, for she came from the ends of the earth to hear the wisdom of Solomon, and behold, something greater than Solomon is here'.

to be too far gone. Since God can take a condemned thief – a wretch – and, in the worst of all conditions, at the lowest of all low points, on the darkest of all dark days, and bring that miserable sinner, at such a time and in such a state, to see – and, I am convinced, to trust – the glorious Christ – if God can do that, then there is hope for you!

Fifthly, I hope this look at the punctuation of Luke 23:43 will encourage us believers, when thinking about the hope we have in Christ, to pay less regard to what is often no more than mere, romantic speculation about the intermediate state, and concentrate, rather, on what Scripture clearly sets before us as our solid hope;[15] namely, the coming of Christ, our resurrection, and entrance into everlasting bliss in Christ's kingdom.

---

[15] Is the lack of confirming testimony from any resurrected people not an issue for those who stress the glories of the intermediate state?

Appendix 3

Calvin on the Resurrection

Because of its valuable contribution to what I have tried to say in this work, I have selected the following from Calvin's *Institutes*.

Calvin was clear that, while the death of Christ was vital in accomplishing the salvation of the elect, this must not be allowed to cloud any emphasis upon his resurrection. He was right.[1]

Calvin:

> Although in [Christ's] death we have an effectual completion of salvation – because by it we are reconciled to God, satisfaction is given to his justice, the curse is removed, and the penalty paid – still it is not by his death, but by his resurrection, that we are said to be begotten [or born] again to a living hope (1 Pet. 1:3); because, as he, by rising again, became victorious over death, so the victory of our faith consists only in his resurrection. The nature of it is better expressed in the words of Paul: 'Who (Christ) was delivered for our offences, and was raised again for our justification' (Rom. 4:25); as if he had said [that] by his death sin was taken away, by his resurrection righteousness was renewed and restored. For how could he, by dying, have freed us from death, if he had yielded to its power? How could he have obtained the victory for us, if he had fallen in the contest? Our salvation may be thus divided between the death and the resurrection of Christ: by the former, sin was abolished and death annihilated; by the latter righteousness was restored and life revived, the power and efficacy of the former being still bestowed upon us by means of the latter. Paul accordingly affirms that he [that is, Christ] was declared to be the Son of God by his resurrection (Rom. 1:4), because he then

---

[1] Read the apostolic sermons in Acts to compare the weight given to Christ's death and his resurrection. I am not trying to play one against the other, but trying to redress my chosen title.

fully displayed that heavenly power which is both a bright mirror of his divinity, and a sure support of our faith; as he also elsewhere teaches, that 'though he was crucified through weakness, yet he lives by the power of God' (2 Cor. 13:4). In the same sense, in another passage [Phil. 3:10], treating of perfection [that is, progressive sanctification – DG], he says: 'That I may know him and the power of his resurrection'. Immediately after he adds, 'being made conformable unto his death'. In perfect accordance with this is the passage in Peter, that God 'raised [Christ] up from the dead, and gave him glory, that your faith and hope might be in God' (1 Pet. 1:21). Not that faith founded merely on his death is vacillating, but that the divine power by which he maintains our faith is most conspicuous in his resurrection.

That, it seems to me, needs emphasis today, certainly more than it gets. I have to plead guilty to being remiss in this aspect of my gospel preaching.

Calvin went on to make a very important point:

Let us remember, therefore, that when [the] death [of Christ] only is mentioned, everything peculiar to the resurrection [of Christ] is at the same time included, and that there is a like *synecdoche* [that is, a part for the whole][2] in the term 'resurrection', as often as it is used apart from death, everything peculiar to death being included. But as, by rising again, [Christ] obtained the victory, and became the resurrection and the life, Paul justly argues: 'If Christ be not raised, your faith is vain; you are yet in your sins' (1 Cor. 15:17). Accordingly, in another passage, after exulting in the death of Christ in opposition to the terrors of condemnation, he thus enlarges: 'Christ that died, indeed rather, that is risen again, who is even at the right hand of God, who also makes intercession for us' (Rom. 8:34).

So much for the importance of the resurrection. Calvin moved on to expand on a vital aspect of all this. As we have just seen, he was clear that the believer's progressive sanctification depends on both the death *and* the resurrection of Christ. He explained further:

---

[2] As an example, take the order: 'All hands on deck!'

Then, as... the mortification of our flesh depends on communion with the cross, so we must also understand that a corresponding benefit is derived from his resurrection. For as the apostle says: 'Like as Christ was raised up from the dead by the glory of the Father, even so we also should walk in newness of life' (Rom. 6:4). Accordingly, as in another passage, from our being dead with Christ, he inculcates: 'Mortify therefore your members which are upon the earth' (Col. 3:5); so from our being risen with Christ he infers: 'Seek those things which are above, where Christ sits at the right hand of God' (Col. 3:1). In these words we are not only urged by the example of a risen Saviour to follow newness of life, but are taught that by his power we are renewed unto righteousness.

Let me stress this because it needs stressing today: Christ's death and resurrection are set before believers, not merely as his saving work, redeeming his people from their sin (which it is, of course), but as empowering them, enabling them not only to know what they should do, but meriting and accomplishing the bestowal of the necessary grace and power for them to do it in Christ (Phil. 4:13), and so 'walk by the Spirit', keeping 'in step with the Spirit' (Gal. 5:16-24).

Calvin continued:

[Another] benefit derived from [Christ's resurrection] is that, like an earnest [that is, a deposit, a pledge, a guarantee], it assures us of our own resurrection, of which it is certain that his is the surest representation. This subject is discussed at length (1 Cor. 15). But it is to be observed, in passing, that when [Christ] is said to have 'risen from the dead', these terms express the reality both of his death and resurrection, as if it had been said that he died the same death as other men naturally die, and received immortality in the same mortal flesh which he had assumed.

I break in once again to stress the point Calvin is making here. The proper rendering of Christ 'having been crucified' (1 Cor. 1:23) is: 'Having been crucified (but he is, of course, now risen)'. The same applies to 'having been crucified' (1 Cor. 2:2). The context is clear: Christ was crucified, yes, certainly, but he is now alive (1 Cor. 1:2,7-9,13,24,30-31); if Christ were still dead, statements affirming that Christ died would be practically meaningless, virtual tautologies, certainly trite. The point is that the emphasis on the death of Christ – proper though that is – must not cloud the fact that he was raised, even when this is not explicitly stated; it is implied. Of course, Scripture does clearly declare it: 'Christ Jesus is the one who died – more than that, who was raised' (Rom. 8:34) and: 'God... raised [Christ] from the dead and gave him glory, so that your faith and hope are in God' (1 Pet. 1:21). But even when the resurrection is not explicitly mentioned, it is never far beneath the surface. That is Calvin's point. And it is a big one.

Calvin went on, taking the link between Christ's death and resurrection even further to include what, judging by the small amount of weight given to it in many circles today, might be seen as the poor relation; namely, Christ's ascension:

The resurrection [of Christ] is naturally followed by [his] ascension into heaven. For although Christ, by rising again, began fully to display his glory and virtue, having laid aside the abject and ignoble condition of a mortal life and the ignominy of the cross, yet it was only by his ascension to heaven that his reign truly commenced. This the apostle shows when he says he ascended 'that he might fill all things' (Eph. 4:10)... Christ, in whom the Father is pleased to be exalted, and by whose hand he is pleased to reign, is said to have been received up, and seated on his right hand (Mark 16:19); as if it had been said, that he was installed in the government of heaven and earth, and formally admitted to possession of the administration committed to him, and not only admitted [as a one-off reception], but to continue until he descends to judgment. For so the apostle interprets [that is, means – DG], when he says that the Father 'set him at his own right hand in the heavenly places, far above all principality, and power, and might, and dominion, and every name that is named not only in this world, but also in that which is to come; and has put all things under his feet, and given him to be the head over all things to the church' [Eph. 1:20-23]. You see to what end he is so seated; namely, that all creatures both in heaven and earth should reverence his majesty, be ruled by his hand, do him implicit homage, and submit to his power. All that the apostles intend, when they so often mention his seat at the Father's hand, is to teach that everything is placed at his disposal. Those, therefore, are in error who suppose that his blessedness merely is indicated [by these words].

That is to say, when we read that Christ is seated in heaven, we are not merely to think of his personal blessedness, but that he has this glorious position of power in order to exercise that power on behalf of his people.[3] As the writer to the Hebrews argued:

> The former [Mosaic, old-covenant] priests were many in number, because they were prevented by death from continuing in office, but he [Jesus] holds his priesthood permanently, because he continues forever. Consequently, he is able to save to the uttermost [that is, at all times] those who draw near to God through him, since he always lives to make intercession for them...
> Christ has entered, not into holy places made with hands, which are copies of the true things, but into heaven itself, now to appear in the presence of God on our behalf (Heb. 7:23-25; 9:24).

As Paul assured the Romans:

> Who shall bring any charge against God's elect? It is God who justifies. Who is to condemn? Christ Jesus is the one who died – more than that, who was raised – who is at the right hand of God, who indeed is interceding for us (Rom. 8:33-34).

Calvin continued to expand on the theme:

> From this doctrine faith derives manifold advantages. *First*, it perceives that the Lord, by his ascension to heaven, has opened up the access to the heavenly kingdom, which Adam had shut. For having entered it in our flesh, as it were in our name, it follows, as the apostle says, that we are in a manner now seated in heavenly places, not entertaining a mere hope of heaven, but possessing it in our Head [Eph. 2:6].

In his ministry, the old-covenant priest had the names of the tribes of Israel inscribed on the garment covering his heart (Ex. 28:29). The new covenant takes this much further. Christ died

---

[3] And more. See, for instance, Matt. 28:18-20.

for, rose for, ascended for, intercedes for his elect by name. As Paul Baynes, preaching on Ephesians, put it, Christ pitches on persons. Christ died for the church, the elect, yes (Eph. 5:25-27), but as Paul put it: 'The Son of God... loved me and gave himself for me' (Gal. 2:20). Similarly, he intercedes for each believer, and will return and raise each believer. Calvin referred to Ephesians 2:6. This verse is part of a massive statement about the believer's present standing and its connection with his eternal hope:

> God, being rich in mercy, because of the great love with which he loved us, even when we were dead in our trespasses, made us alive together with Christ – by grace you have been saved – and raised us up with him and seated us with him in the heavenly places in Christ Jesus, so that in the coming ages he might show the immeasurable riches of his grace in kindness toward us in Christ Jesus (Eph. 2:4-7).

All this carries enormous consequences, some of which Calvin set out. Opening with a glorious understatement, he went on:

> *Secondly*, faith perceives that [Christ's] seat beside the Father is not without great advantage to us. Having entered the temple not made with hands, he constantly appears as our advocate and intercessor in the presence of the Father; directs attention to his own righteousness, so as to turn it away from our sins; so reconciles him to us, as by his intercession to pave for us a way of access to his throne, presenting it to miserable sinners, to whom it would otherwise be an object of dread, as replete with grace and mercy. *Thirdly*, it discerns [that is, displays] his power, on which depend our strength, might, resources, and triumph over hell: 'When he ascended up on high, he led captivity captive' (Eph. 4:8). Spoiling his foes, he gave gifts to his people, and daily loads them with spiritual riches. He thus occupies his exalted seat, that thence transferring his virtue unto us, he may quicken us to spiritual life, sanctify us by his Spirit, and adorn his church with various graces, by his protection preserve it safe from all harm, and by the strength of his hand curb the enemies raging against his cross and our salvation; *in fine*, that he may possess all power in heaven and earth, until he have utterly routed all his foes, who are also ours, and completed the structure of his church. Such is the true nature of the kingdom, such the power which the Father has

conferred upon him, until he arrive to complete the last act by judging the living and the dead.

Of course, the kingdom is not here on earth in its fullness at present. Indeed, 'the whole world lies in the power of the evil one' (1 John 5:19). Nevertheless, much as it may not seem like it at present, believers see – by faith – that Christ truly is King. They know that 'the reason the Son of God appeared was to destroy the works of the devil' (1 John 3:8). Moreover, as he said at the return of the seventy-two: 'I saw Satan fall like lightning from heaven' (Luke 10:18). Believers are convinced of the truth of Christ's assertions just before his death: 'Now is the judgment of this world; now will the ruler of this world be cast out' (John 12:31) and 'the ruler of this world is judged' (John 16:11). They know that Christ has 'all power' (Matt. 28:18-20).

Calvin:

> Christ, indeed, gives his followers no dubious proofs of present power, but, as his kingdom in the world is in a manner veiled by the humiliation of a carnal condition, faith is most properly invited to meditate on the visible presence which he will exhibit on the last day. For he will descend from heaven in visible form, in like manner as he was seen to ascend, and appear to all, with the ineffable majesty of his kingdom, the splendour of immortality, the boundless power of divinity, and an attending company of angels. Hence we are told to wait for the Redeemer against that day on which he will separate the sheep from the goats, and the elect from the reprobate, and when not one individual either of the living or the dead shall escape his judgment. From the extremities of the universe shall be heard the clang [better – the blast – DG] of the trumpet summoning all to his tribunal; both those whom that day shall find alive, and those whom death shall previously have removed from the society of the living... Though no one can deny that that destruction of the flesh will be death, it still remains true that the living and the dead shall be summoned to judgment (1 Thess. 4:16); for 'the dead in Christ shall rise first; then we which are alive and remain shall be caught up together with them in the clouds to meet the Lord in the air'... (Acts 10:42)... (2 Tim. 4:1).
> It is most consolatory to think, that judgment is vested in him who has already destined us to share with him in the honour of

judgment (Matt. 19:28); so far is it from being true, that he will ascend the judgment seat for our condemnation. How could a most merciful Prince destroy his own people? How could the Head disperse its own members? How could the advocate condemn his clients? For if the apostle, when contemplating the interposition of Christ, is bold to exclaim: 'Who is he that condemns?' (Rom. 8:33), much more certain is it that Christ, the intercessor, will not condemn those whom he has admitted to his protection. ['Who shall bring any charge against God's elect? It is God who justifies. Who is to condemn? Christ Jesus is the one who died – more than that, who was raised – who is at the right hand of God, who indeed is interceding for us' (Rom. 8:33-34).]... *In fine*, since in him all kinds of blessings are treasured up, let us draw a full supply from him, and none from any other quarter. Those who, not satisfied with him alone, entertain various hopes from others, though they may continue to look to him chiefly, deviate from the right path by the simple fact that some portion of their thought takes a different direction. No distrust of this description can arise when once the abundance of his blessings is properly known.

Again:

None participate in the benefits of Christ save those who raise their minds to the resurrection... In order that he may stimulate us the more powerfully, [the writer to the Hebrews speaks of] the final advent of Christ our redemption. It is true, indeed, that all the parts of our redemption are already accomplished; but as Christ was once offered for sins (Heb. 9:28), so he shall again appear without sin unto salvation. Whatever, then, be the afflictions by which we are pressed, let this redemption sustain us until its final accomplishment. The very importance of the subject ought to increase our ardour. Paul justly contends, that if Christ rise not the whole gospel is delusive and vain (1 Cor. 15:13-17); for our condition would be more miserable than that of other mortals, because we are exposed to much hatred and insult, and incur danger every hour – indeed, [we] are like sheep destined for slaughter – and hence the authority of the gospel would fail, not in one part merely, but in its very essence, including both our adoption and the accomplishment of our salvation. Let us, therefore, give heed to a matter of all others the most serious, so that no length of time may produce weariness.

Of course, it is all a question of faith, and – as we all have to confess – our faith is not always strong. Calvin acknowledged this:

It is difficult to believe that after our bodies have been consumed with rottenness, they will rise again at their appointed time... To enable faith to surmount the great difficulty, Scripture furnishes two auxiliary proofs, the one the likeness of Christ's resurrection, and the other the omnipotence of God. Therefore, whenever the subject of the resurrection is considered, let us think of the case of our Saviour, who, having completed his mortal course in our nature which he had assumed, obtained immortality, and is now the pledge of our future resurrection... Hence Paul's argument: 'If there be no resurrection of the dead, then is Christ not risen' (1 Cor. 15:13); for he assumes it as an acknowledged principle that when Christ was subjected to death, and by rising gained a victory over death, it was not on his own account, but in the Head was begun what must necessarily be fulfilled in all the members.

Let me close this Appendix by repeating this invaluable caution for believers from Calvin:

To pry curiously into their intermediate state is neither lawful nor expedient... It is foolish and rash to inquire into hidden things, farther than God permits us to know... What teacher or doctor will reveal to us what God has concealed?... Since Scripture uniformly enjoins us to look with expectation to the [second] advent of Christ, and delays the crown of glory till that period, let us be contented with the limits divinely prescribed to us – that is, that the souls of the righteous, after their warfare is ended, obtain blessed rest where in joy they wait for the fruition of promised glory, and that thus the final result is suspended till Christ the Redeemer appears.

Wise words.